YOUR TOTAL WEALTH

This book will become a classic. It is a must read for anyone who wants to make his or her money work for him or her over time. Topics are presented in bite size pieces, allowing the reader to pick up and put down the book to fit the available time. If you know someone who needs time-honored investment knowledge, suggest this book or provide it as a gift. It will also be appreciated by any experienced investor seeking assurance that he or she is on the right track to build wealth while keeping life in balance.

Jack P. Friedman, PhD, CPA/ABV, MAI. Former university professor, financial and real estate consultant, editor, co-author of 30 books including best-selling business dictionaries and the 2nd edition of Encyclopedia of Investments.

In the book, Your Total Wealth, Lyle and David have written a nuanced way to better increase your financial literacy. Their emphasis on finding the balance between the financial and the soulful - that which provides happiness - marks the growing need for understanding financial planning is not just about finances, but so much more. The authors are able to teach on a whole host of financial topics through relatable examples that show how the financial intersects with the behavioral, psychological, emotional, and relational. Financial professionals, as well as anyone interested in increasing their balance between finances and life, will find the lessons in this book beneficial.

Bruce Ross, Ph.D., Assistant Professor, Department of Family Science, University of Kentucky, and President of the Financial Therapy Association.

Sussman and Dubofsky have outdone themselves! Ingeniously, the authors write a glossary of quotes and vignettes linking financial wealth terms to "total wealth" life advice. Thoughtful quotes help us balance the yin of building financial wealth with the yang of building emotional ties or spiritual wealth. Each definition and financial term hooks you with wonderful quotes, epigrams and stories. Uniquely, the authors dispense wry and dry wit with sage advice that shine through each page. The day to change your total wealth enhancing choices is today (yes, procrastination is addressed as well). Start with buying a copy of Sussman and Dubofsky, flip open the book to the life advice quote by Hank Aaron, and just keep swinging!

James A. Conover, PhD, CFP®, CFE, CMA, CTP; investor; consultant; LuminDX comptroller; and Emeritus Professor of Finance, University of North Texas.

Sussman and Dubofsky do a masterful job of breathing life into the presumed dead subject of financial literacy by introducing personal fulfillment into the matter. Your Total Wealth makes financial literacy organic. It makes financial literacy into a living, breathing and evolving matter. (If chemistry can be made organic, why can't financial literacy?)

Scott E. Hein, PhD, Emeritus Professor of Finance, Texas Tech University; Independent Board Member at FinPro Inc.; Financial Author, Consultant, Investor and Researcher; Lecturer at state and national schools of banking; Former Advisor and Senior, Economist, Federal Reserve System.

Having taught finance and economics for more than forty years, I appreciate not only the need for financial knowledge but also how challenging the subject can be. Your Total Wealth by Sussman and Dubofsky does an excellent job of achieving their goal of simplifying financial concepts without creating undue complexity. One underlying theme of the book is to go beyond the math of finance and help the reader understand that financial concepts are a means to an end. The authors stress the importance of focusing on the why of achieving the reader's own unique set of financial goals. The authors approach is refreshing. What's more it comes at a time when we all need to address financial literacy to help achieve our goals of financial and personal enrichment.

S. Scott MacDonald PhD is president and CEO of the Southwestern Graduate School of Banking at SMU, director of the Assemblies for Bank Directors, and Adjunct Professor of Finance, Cox School of Business, Southern Methodist University. He is author of articles in professional and academic journals as well as co-author of the college textbook on banking, *Bank Management*.

Finally, someone comes along and takes all those technical financial issues that individuals need to understand about building wealth and puts real life into our thought process. Your Total Wealth's constant interactions of financial considerations along with applications toward a more meaningful life help us realize that we all need to re-assess the consistency and balance between our financial pursuits and our personal, family, and spiritual lives. Here we have the

Don Meredith color commentary to Howard Cosell's "Tell it like it is" play by play, and the result first helps you understand more financial areas, and then makes you think more expansively about where your values (should) lie. The year 2020 has provided the perfect incentive to read this book.

Randall S James, President Randall S. James and Associates. University Lecturer, banking consultant, advisor to banking schools and university banking programs, regulatory liaison, former Texas State Banking Commissioner.

"Your Total Wealth" is a delicious meal for the mind and the soul. It never loses sight of the main purpose of personal wealth management – to provide for future needs and happiness. It serves its knowledge in easy digestible pieces, with short explanations put into the context of the overall financial picture. The book is a great guide for people who want to dive into an article in the financial press and understand the specifics. It's also a good primer before one decides on a financial advisor.

Scott Lummer, PhD, CFA, CEO of Savant Investment Group, LLC and award-winning playwright.

Finance as a basis for teaching life lessons? Really? Amazingly, Your Total Wealth does just that. For example, consider this simple idea that Lyle Sussman and David Dubofsky present: "budgets … are a comparison between what you could do with what you must do." This is a life lesson for both an individual and a corporation. Balancing work and life and realizing that financial gain can have a heart and soul is a lesson for us all.

Joel Naroff PhD, is President of Naroff Economics LLC, author and multiple award winning economist. He has been quoted in *Business Week, The Wall Street Journal, USA Today, Financial Times* and *Newsweek,* with frequent appearances on CNBC, Fox Business News, and Bloomberg Television.

YOUR TOTAL WEALTH

THE HEART AND SOUL OF FINANCIAL LITERACY

Lyle Sussman PhD and David Dubofsky PhD, CFA

HSF Publishing LLC
Dover, Delaware

Printed in the United States of America.

Library of Congress Cataloging-in-Publication Data:
Sussman, Lyle, 1944- author. | Dubofsky, David A., author.
Your total wealth : the heart and soul of financial literacy / Lyle Sussman, PhD, and David Dubofsky, PhD, CFA.
Includes bibliographical references and index.

ISBN-13 for paperback edition: **978-1-7356165-0-6**
ISBN-10 for paperback edition: **1735616508**
ISBN for e-book: **978-1-7356165-1-3**

LCSH: Finance, Personal. | Financial literacy. | Wealth.
Classification: LCC HG179 .S87 2021 (print) | LCC HG179 (e-book) | DDC 332.024--dc23

2020922000

To

My wonderful and loving wife, Paulette.
The memory of my parents, Harry and Celia.
And all my friends and family.

— D.A.D.

To

Suzy, you are my wealth.

— L.S.

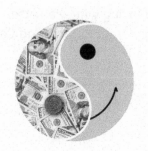

CONTENTS

ACKNOWLEDGEMENTS

We are grateful to Lee Chottiner for his careful proofreading and editing of the book, Eric V. Van Der Hope for his help in getting through the logistics of publishing, Stephanie Meyers for her design work, Jacob Pawlak for creating our webpage, and Jen Henderson for formatting. Jack Friedman and Nikita Perumal provided useful comments on the content. Nicholas Block, David Davis, Candace Bernard, Dennis Beaver and Bob Glickman also provided valuable advice.

YIN AND YANG
OF PERSONAL FINANCE

SUCCESS IS GETTING WHAT YOU WANT.
HAPPINESS IS WANTING WHAT YOU GET.
— *Dale Carnegie*

Imagine for a moment that you are in a large room filled with financial planners. They are not like your Uncle Harry or Cousin Sally, who pride themselves on being financially savvy, periodically giving you hot stock tips and advice on managing your credit cards.

No, these are *professional planners,* who devote 40-60 hours a week to clients willing and able to pay for advice on managing wealth and creating financial peace of mind. Many are professionally credentialed financial advisors.

Walking around the room, casually listening to the chatter, you hope to pick up hot investment tips on the cheap. But you hear nothing of the sort, nothing about stocks poised to double in price, strategies for smart asset allocations, economic forecasts, or the latest rumors on Wall Street.

To your surprise, these planners are sharing anecdotes that could be story lines for some TV soap opera. These are the real stories from the financial-planning trenches: personal anecdotes about the heart-wrenching issues their clients are facing, vignettes of human drama and frailty.

As if a light were turned on, you are presented with firsthand confirmation that wealth solves some problems, but not all of them. In fact, it may *create* problems. At once, the devastating truth of the Midas touch parable becomes clear: a passionate and obsessive quest for gold may get you gold, but it exacts a too-high price – anguish, heartache, family decay, spiritual poverty.

Welcome to the true workings of financial planning.

A few years ago, we conducted a study with the support of the Financial Planning Association. ♪ We explored the changing role of financial planners, from one focusing exclusively on financial analytics and money management to one encompassing coaching and life planning.

We obtained anonymous and confidential data from a sample of 1,384 financial planners. Seventy five percent of the sample were responsible for managing over $20 million of their clients' financial assets. The results of this study have been cited in professional journals, summarized at professional conferences, and incorporated into the financial-planning curricula at many colleges and universities.

What we found supports the time-honored truism that personal wealth may come with unintended consequences. The only problem that money will assuredly and unequivocally solve is that of *not* having money. As Johnny Cash said, *"Success is having to worry about every damn thing in the world except money."*

Suicide, depression, addictions, divorce, family turmoil, terminal illness, chronic physical pain, emotional pain, the soul-searching quest for spirituality; this is a list of personal distress you would expect priests, ministers, rabbis, imams, therapists, and professional care givers to wrestle with – not financial planners. Yet our study found financial planners do confront these issues. After all, they are serving human beings who have human problems.

Today, financial planners are challenged to listen to their clients with empathy before offering advice. And when the time comes to counsel, they must go beyond financial algorithms, computer simulations and economic forecasts. Our research shows that possessing quantitative skills – knowing the lay of the economic land – while necessary for serving clients, is not nearly enough to satisfy their human needs and desires.

YIN OF FINANCE, YANG OF PERSONAL FULFILLMENT

This distinction between necessary and sufficient is the premise of our book. It is the logic underlying the yin-yang title of this introduction. Based on ancient Chinese philosophy, the yin and the yang connote the complementary, harmonious fusion of seemingly opposite forces. For example, consider these opposing yet complementary forces: activity and rest, sunrise and sunset, seasonal cycles, oriental martial arts, and yes, financial wealth coupled with psychological and physical health.

The give and take between aggression and submission, active and passive, is the essence of the yin and the yang. Natural forces, according to this philosophy, are not in destructive conflict, but rather *constructive growth,* resulting in a harmonious whole. Our ability to experience peace and fulfillment is tempered by having lived through turmoil and loss.

Do we need money to survive? Of course, we do. Will financial literacy, understanding the essence of financial management, increase our ability to cope in an increasingly complex world? Yes, it will. But is money all we need to feel fulfilled? Is it sufficient to meet our emotional and psychological needs? That question is answered in the proverb, "Money can't buy happiness."

Financial planning thus requires a yin-yang blending of the necessary and sufficient, of the complementary needs, of the financial and soulful, to create a harmonious whole.

And so, we have a powerful lens for viewing and reconciling the duality of acquiring financial wealth while seeking personal growth and fulfillment. Dale Carnegie's penetrating insight, "Success is getting what you want. Happiness is wanting what you get," is a testament to the quest for balancing the financial-personal fulfillment duality.

Other writers have stressed the importance of achieving riches without filing for spiritual bankruptcy. They see the Midas touch as a parable that could have been written by Stephen King.

The message of this book supports those writers, but it adds a distinctive, epiphany-inducing format. Financial wealth and personal fulfillment are not mutually exclusive. The quest for a healthy balance need not result in a zero-sum tragedy. A yin-yang harmony creates your *total wealth*, and that glorious fusion is not only possible, but required for defining the full richness of your life and for achieving your full potential. Our goal in this book is to help you achieve that potential.

OUR YIN-YANG FORMAT

You *can* acquire wealth without selling your soul. We help you achieve that goal by explaining basic financial concepts – the foundations of financial literacy – while framing those concepts in the context of balance, growth and personal fulfillment. To highlight the duality of financial well-being with psychological and spiritual well-being, we examine financial literacy juxtaposed with reflections on humanity.

This book creates a bridge between money and fulfillment, one built on the foundation of moving from a false dichotomy of either/or to a fusion of and/also, from zero-sum to sum. In the pages that follow, you will see a complementary duality: the yin – definitions, examples and prescriptions for acquiring financial literacy – immediately followed by the yang – insights and recommendation for achieving personal fulfillment, conceptually linked to that financial literacy.

Defining and providing examples of some of the yins required cross referencing with other yins. When you see an underlined term, realize that it has its own dedicated yin. Financial literacy incorporates multiple interrelated concepts. Simple cross referencing helps you understand those relationships. We also included a Notes section at the back of the book, not because we are obsessive academics, but because a few of the yins called for an expanded example, or tips for further application. A note (♪) at the end of a yin signifies additional discussion. You will find them helpful.

HOW TO READ THIS BOOK

You have multiple options for reading and using this book. The financial terms are presented in four chapters, but the sequence in which you read the terms is up to you. We recommend beginning with the first term (Finance) and reading sequentially until you read the last term (Financial Wealth).

We expect many will choose that option. But because the terms may be studied independently, you could scan the Table of Contents and pick and choose terms of greatest interest, terms representing issues that are most pressing or urgent, or even choose terms randomly.

Regardless how you read this book we are convinced the definitions, examples, lessons, quotes, vignettes, and cross referencing will draw you in. You will then have a different perspective of *Your Total Wealth*, regardless of your financial savvy or size of your portfolio.

Finally, we ask you to open your mind, your heart and your soul to our message. Yes, some of the financial concepts might appear intimidating at first, especially if finance and numbers were never your thing. All of us feel intimidated and insecure when stepping out of our comfort zone. But soon, you will see how financial security and personal fulfillment are within your grasp.

With your heart, mind, and soul open, you now begin a journey to increase your financial literacy. And because you will overcome intimidation and insecurity, you realize, in the words of Eric Hofer, *"The hardest arithmetic to master is that which enables us to count our blessings."*

CHAPTER 1

THE FOUNDATION OF FINANCIAL LITERACY

To increase your financial literacy, you must first understand the basics and the often confusing jargon of finance. This understanding also includes recognizing the ever-changing external, environmental forces affecting how you manage your money. Learning the terms and their related implications that follow will help you adapt to those forces more wisely while building a portfolio of financial and personal enrichment.

FINANCE

Well, what exactly is finance? We define it as a set of concepts, rules and theories concerning how to best raise and use money.

By "raising money," we mean the judicious borrowing of money, by consumers like you, to fund consumption; the taxation and borrowing by governments to pay for their expenditures; and the raising of <u>capital</u> by businesses, often by borrowing from banks or issuing <u>bonds</u>, and selling ownership shares (<u>stock</u>, or equity).

By "using money," we mean planning expenditures, like buying an affordable home or <u>insurance</u> policy, or making savings and investment decisions concerning stocks, bonds, etc.

An investment requires the commitment of your money with the hope that you will be repaid with more money in the future. Investments can be riskless (insured bank CDs or U.S. government treasury securities) or <u>risky</u> (meaning you can lose money; stocks are quite risky because stock prices can decline). Often, buying short-term, riskless investments such as insured bank savings accounts is called "saving" rather than "investing."

Governments spending money on infrastructure, education or services for people in need is another form of investment.

Businesses deciding what products to make, services to provide and property or equipment to buy also are making investments, also known as capital expenditures.

For individuals, it's called "personal finance"; for governments, "public finance"; for businesses, "business finance," "corporate finance" or "financial management."

THE LESSON

"A fool and his money are soon parted." Pay attention to the basic financial knowledge we are providing in this book. Don't over-borrow. Don't over-spend. Save an appropriate amount for your retirement. Be aware of the risks you are taking. Read books on finance. Visit the websites we list in our closing notes to this book to learn more. Pay attention to what is happening in the economy and in financial markets. Above all, focus on the big picture: How best to raise and use your money to achieve *total wealth*. ♪

Whether you use checks, a debit card or credit card, you receive a monthly statement of everything you purchased during that period, excluding cash purchases. That statement is a time-bound "snapshot" of how you used money.

But suppose at the end of your life you had the magical power to look at thousands of your snapshots? What is the "big picture" and what would it reveal?

The big picture would reveal the relative percentage of money you spent on immediate consumption instead of investment for the future. Were you focused on here and now, or were you planning for all your future tomorrows?

The big picture would reveal the relative percentage of money you spent to maintain body and soul. Did you contribute to any religious or charitable causes? Did you spend money to maintain your physical health? Were you your brother's keeper?

The big picture would reveal whether you were always catching up with your creditors or whether you were taking a debt-free journey through life. Were creditors chasing you or were you chasing a dream?

Finally, it would reveal your dreams, aspirations, values and beliefs. Those thousands of monthly statements would say less about what you say about how you want to live your life than how you *actually* lived your life.

That big picture would tell the world what wealth really meant to you.

You are creating those monthly statements right now – as you live and breathe. You have the power to turn those statements into the big picture that will make you and your loved ones proud.

We wish you heart, soul, and wisdom in creating that picture.

BALANCE SHEET

A physical exam monitors vital signs: pulse, weight, blood pressure, lungs. If you wanted to examine the financial health of a company, you would study its vital signs; the balance sheet provides some of this information.

A balance sheet is a financial statement that presents everything a company currently owns (assets, on the left-hand side) and everything owed (liabilities, on the right-hand side). The balance sheet is a snapshot taken at one point in time. Of course, we hope that there is a positive difference between assets and liabilities (i.e., assets greater than liabilities), and this difference is known as net worth, owners' equity or stockholders' equity. Thus assets = liabilities + owners' equity. This simple equation is called the most basic equation in accounting.

The balance sheet always balances; no matter what a firm does, no matter what transaction it makes, assets will always equal liabilities plus owners' equity. This is the basis of double-entry accounting.

If you invest in individual stocks, it will be worth your while to learn how to read a corporation's balance sheet (as well as its other financial statements). It will reveal several characteristics of the corporation and whether the company is worth your investment. A good balance sheet, one that depicts positive performance, will display liquidity (the ability to meet short-term obligations), reasonable leverage (acceptable amounts of debt) and positive net worth.

Financial statements can be accessed at several websites. Enter the name or ticker symbol of the company in which you are interested, then find the most recent 10-Q or 10-K report. Google the term "reading financial statements" to find websites that explain how to read financial statements.

THE LESSON

You reduce financial risk by increasing your knowledge. How would you know if you should invest in a company? Analyzing its balance sheet increases your knowledge and reduces your risk. Secondly, you can use the balance sheet model to prepare your own personal balance sheet. What are your assets? What are your liabilities? Do you have positive net worth? Strive to increase your own personal net worth, and monitor changes in your personal balance sheet changes over time.

> *IF YOU DON'T ADMIT A MISTAKE AND TAKE RESPONSIBILITY FOR IT, YOU'RE BOUND TO MAKE THE SAME ONE AGAIN.*
> *— Pat Summitt*

There are multiple reasons why we take the time and incur the cost of measuring something. One reason is we simply want to take a current read: how is something going? Another reason is we want to compare readings over time: how does this read compare to past reads? A third reason is formal laws or regulations mandate the read: this read is in compliance.

But there is a fourth reason. Measuring and monitoring forces us to answer the "so what?" question. Things are going well, so what do we do to make sure that doesn't change? Things are growing poorly, so what do we do to turn it around? Things are going so-so, so what do we do to get off center? Answering the "so what" question is the essence of accountability.

Go to school on Pat Summitt's call for accountability. Collecting data for a balance sheet (or for a personal statement of net worth) is a fool's errand unless you are prepared to answer the "so what?" question. Accountability is a sign of strength, maturity, and a willingness to grow and improve.

In her 38 years as head coach of the University of Tennessee women's basketball team, Summitt never had a losing season, and she won 1,098 games. She retired as the winningest basketball coach, male or female, in NCAA history. She measured, monitored, and held herself accountable.

You better believe she was continually answering the "so what?" question. Do not measure and monitor if you don't have the courage to answer that question.

ASSETS

If you borrow money, your lender will likely ask you for a list of your assets and their values. An asset is something you own or can use because you are in the process of paying for or leasing it. You may borrow to buy a car, or lease it, and it is still your asset even though you don't actually own it, but you do have its use.

Assets may be tangible (real estate, cars, furniture, jewelry) or intangible (your knowledge or reputation). Assets also have value. Here, we discuss assets with monetary value, not necessarily their intrinsic value. You may love your furniture or believe that your grandmother's tea set is priceless. Those feelings are intrinsic. But a tangible asset has monetary value in an exchange between a buyer and seller.

Corporate assets are reported in a financial statement called a <u>balance sheet</u>. There are two sides to the balance sheet: the right side lists <u>liabilities</u> (what is owed) and the left side lists assets and their estimated cost. Cash, securities, inventory, accounts receivable (payments from customers the firm is waiting for – sort of like IOUs), prepaid items such as rent, real estate and property are all typical assets that appear on a balance sheet.

Many firms also own intangible assets. The most common intangible asset is called goodwill, which usually arises when accountants determine that the firm excessively paid (according to accounting rules) for an acquisition of another company.

THE LESSON

Apply the corporate balance sheet model to your personal finances. But also recognize that you have more assets than you think you have. Prepare the left hand side of your own personal balance sheet. Start by listing your house, car, furniture, jewelry, electronics, clothing, investments, etc. If your tangible assets are extensive and difficult to value, you may want to hire a professional (a credentialed appraiser) trained in estimating the value of <u>illiquid</u> and hard-to-value assets. But you will only get an "estimate." *Then*, add all your intangible assets. Finally, remember a tea set that is priceless *does* have a price.

> *YOU AREN'T WEALTHY UNTIL YOU HAVE*
> *SOMETHING MONEY CAN'T BUY.*
> *— Garth Brooks*

Obituaries, regardless of the gender and ethnicity of the deceased, have common elements: name, age, date and place of death, surviving loved ones and possibly a picture. Depending on the age of the deceased, the obituary may list names of parents and siblings who preceded in death plus the deceased's formal education, occupation, and noteworthy awards or accomplishments.

Again, depending on age you are likely to see a statement about the person's hobbies or a heart-warming anecdote. At some point, in most cases, you will see a statement similar to, "passed away with family at the bedside." Such a statement speaks to the richness of a person's life and the *real* legacy that he or she leaves behind.

Across the ages, philosophers and theologians have drawn a distinction between wealth defined by tangible assets and wealth defined by spiritual pursuits and familial bonds. This resoundingly clear message communicates what too many learn too late: *Money in the absence of family is spiritual poverty; family in the absence of money is spiritual wealth.*

The advice on the previous page is important. If it wasn't, we wouldn't waste our time writing it, or ask you to waste your time reading it. But the advice on this page is equally, if not more, important.

Finally, revisit all the obituaries you have read and think about those you may have helped to write. None of those contained this sentence: "Accountants, bankers and financial advisors were at the bedside."

LIABILITIES

A liability is something that you owe. All debts are liabilities. But some liabilities may not be debts.

You probably have several liabilities, including credit card debt, auto loans and mortgages. If you signed a lease, you have a liability. Maybe you have bought stock on margin; this creates a liability for you.

If you start a sole proprietorship or a general partnership as a business, you will have unlimited liability, which means that you personally must pay what the business owes. A limited liability company (LLC) provides a significant advantage if you start a business. As its name suggests, the members of an LLC have limited liability. The stockholders in a corporation are the owners, their liability limited only to what they invested in the company.

Corporate liabilities include accounts payable (the company bought something, but hasn't paid for it), wages payable (the firm's employees have worked, but haven't been paid yet), bonds and leases.

A liability that will be paid off within a year is called a "current liability." Long term liabilities need not be repaid for longer periods of time. The difference between current assets (assets that will be converted to cash within a year) and current liabilities is called "working capital." The difference between total assets and total liabilities is called net worth, or stockholders' equity.

A warranty is a liability requiring the seller to repair or replace the item under warranty, if it is defective.

THE LESSON

A reasonable amount of liabilities is not a bad thing. Borrowing to buy a home (a mortgage) gives you an asset and a place to live, but it also creates two liabilities: the mortgage itself and a potential liability if someone has an accident on your property due to your negligence. If you need transportation, an auto loan to buy a car may be necessary, but you will need to buy liability insurance in case you injure someone while driving, or cause property damage with your car. Credit card debt makes life easier, but you must pay your bills on time or risk getting hit with high interest charges. Manage your liabilities carefully. Be sure you can pay them off and satisfy your obligations and promises on time.

> *DON'T LET YOUR MOUTH WRITE*
> *A CHECK YOUR TAIL CAN'T CASH.*
> *— Bo Diddley*

Of course, Bo is talking about the kind of check you write with your mouth, not with a pen. He may mean having to back up your threats if necessary, but he also is saying something about promises in general. In no uncertain terms, he is telling us not to promise what we can't deliver.

When you say you will do something, you are creating an expectation. You are implicitly saying that you can be trusted. And if you use the word "promise," you are explicitly pledging to deliver. You will necessarily be held accountable.

A promise is an obligation; you owe that person what you promised to deliver. Therefore, a promise is a debt – based on money or something else. When you deliver on that promise, you have paid the debt. Good for you.

But suppose you default. Suppose you break that promise. What then?

There are prices to be paid for breaking promises. Here is what you stand to lose:

Credibility: Your word is no longer your bond. Any future promises you make will be discounted or dismissed by those whose trust you violate. Once you lose credibility your life becomes harder. People no longer cut you slack; they don't give you the benefit of the doubt.

Bonding and Relationships: When others no longer cut you slack, and doubt your word, relationships regress to simple quid pro quo transactions. Your words no longer serve as currency; others only accept your deeds as payment.

You can still have relationships after you default on your promises, but they will lack heart and soul; they will be purely transactional.

Here's to Bo for telling it like is.

INCOME STATEMENT

An income statement is a summary of a firm's financial performance during a period such as a quarter or a year. It presents the dollar amounts of revenues and expenses; the difference between them is called profit or net income.

Here is a simplified version of Apple's income statement for 2019 (in millions of dollars... Yes, their revenues were $260 billion!):

sales revenues	$260,174
- expenses	$194,437
Taxable income	$65,737
- income taxes	$10,481
Net income	$55,256

Revenues include both cash and credit sales of goods and services. Because of credit sales, a firm may not actually receive all of its revenues in cash. This is one reason that net income is not the same as a cash flow.

There are several types of expenses:

- Cost of goods sold includes the costs of raw materials, labor and other expenses to produce goods that were sold. Some of these costs are credit purchases, and others are paid for with cash.
- Selling, general and administrative expenses, sometimes called "overhead," include expenses unrelated to production (e.g., marketing and management).
- Depreciation and amortization expense, which are noncash expenses.
- Interest expense.
- Income tax expense.

After all expenses are deducted from revenues, we are left with net income, or profit, which is often called "the bottom line" of the income statement. If you divide net income by the number of shares of stock outstanding, you get earnings per share, EPS, which measures the profit earned per share of common stock.

THE LESSON

Firms with growing profits are generally worthy of investment. As profitability increases, so will the company's stock price. When corporations announce unexpectedly high earnings, their stock prices often rise. But prices can drop if disappointing earnings are announced. If you take out a loan from a bank, you may be asked to create your own income statement so that your lender has a bottom line assessment of the potential risk you present.

*TAKE LESS TIME TO READ THE SCORECARD
AND MORE TIME TO READ THE HOLE.*
— Chi Chi Rodriguez

An income statement is a scorecard.

As we go through life, your performance shows up on many scorecards. You receive grades in school, results of lab tests during an annual physical, a yearly accounting of income reported to the IRS, final scores in any athletic events you might enter, and possibly an annual performance evaluation where you work.

All scorecards share a common characteristic: They describe performance with an assigned number. That number results in evaluative assessment. Was performance good or bad? How did the performance compare to that of others? Did the performance improve or decline?

But there is a downside to assessing performance based on numerical scores. The score represents the performance; it is *not* the actual performance.

Your grade point average in school doesn't tell anyone about the sleepless nights you spent to meet deadlines. Your score in a tennis match or bowling league doesn't mention your sore feet or pulled muscles. And income statements don't address the blood, sweat and tears (or lack thereof) that produced those numbers. They, like all scorecards are abstractions – inferences about reality.

The difference between measuring performance and the actual performance highlights the power of Chi Chi's advice.

If you are judging a company's or person's performance based on a number, take into account the humanity behind the number – the heart and soul of performance.

Also, if your performance will be assessed with a number, make sure you focus on performing to your best ability. Focus on doing your very best at the task at hand. Do your very best now. The number will take care of itself.

Focus on the hole (and the whole), not the scorecard.

DEPRECIATION

Economic depreciation is a decline in an <u>asset</u>'s value. It is often said that a new car depreciates in value by 10-15 percent as soon as you drive it off the lot; if you tried to sell it the day after you bought it, you would likely receive only 85-90 percent of what you paid for it. Such is the difference between retail prices (what you paid) and market values (what you would receive).

Businesses depreciate the <u>capital</u> equipment they buy. For example, if a newspaper pays $1 million for a printing press, it only recognizes a fraction of that amount as an annual expense on its <u>income statement</u>. This rule exists because the machinery is likely to be used for several years, and the depreciation expense reflects the gradual loss in value over its useful life. This is consistent with what accountants often call "the matching principle," which is to match costs with related revenues.

Just as depreciation expense is spread out over several years on its income statement, the firm also recognizes depreciation as a tax-<u>deductible</u> expense. Often, the rate at which equipment is depreciated on income statements differs from the rate used to depreciate the item for tax purposes. The rules for accounting depreciation may be very different from the true decline in value. In other words, accounting depreciation is different from economic depreciation.

If you use a home office for business, then you can depreciate that part of your personal residence, and this will lower your income taxes. But be careful; IRS rules about depreciating a home office, and the tax consequences when you later sell your home, are very precise.

THE LESSON

If you operate a business, understand how depreciation affects your taxes and the market value of that business if you choose to sell. Even if you don't own a business, depreciation also affects your personal financial planning. Determining your net worth, deciding how to distribute assets to your heirs, and simply tracking your net worth over time will all be affected by your assets' depreciation. It would be wonderful if everything you owned increased in value over time (appreciation), but that wonder only exists in fairytales.

> *THE DEEPEST PRINCIPLE IN HUMAN NATURE*
> *IS THE CRAVING TO BE APPRECIATED.*
> — *William James*

You depreciate a possession by following accounting rules and regulations. Depreciation, in that sense, is purely economic. You can also *appreciate* a possession. For example, you may have a strong emotional connection to your car, your piano, a favorite reading lamp, even your riding lawn mower. Appreciation in that sense is not economic, but psychological or emotional.

You can also appreciate people. You may love your spouse, parents and children, and are sincerely thankful for the joy they bring to your life. Similarly, you may appreciate your customers and your co-workers, who brighten your day. You may even work for one of the many companies that tell the world how its employees are its most important resource.

But appreciating others and having them *feel* appreciated are two different things. You may sincerely believe you appreciate your spouse and that your actions show it. But your spouse may have a totally different perspective, believing that you care more about a physical possession than you do about him or her.

Likewise, telling an employee, "you are valued, and we appreciate having you here," may or may not be validated by what that employee feels. In fact, you may be one of the many employees who believe that their company hypocritically announces the value of human resources while showing far greater concern for every machine it has, from its computers to its delivery vans.

Feeling appreciated is a basic human need. Don't announce your appreciation unless you are willing to show it. You can never break a machine's heart, but you can break a person's heart.

CASH FLOW

Ever hear the term, "Cash is king"? Cash flow is what it implies: cash inflow minus cash outflow. It's the number of dollars received less the dollars paid out.

If a firm paid out $100 in cash yesterday while simultaneously receiving $120 in cash, then it had a cash inflow of $20. Net income is not a cash flow. Accounting profit is not a cash flow. In fact, many companies have reported positive net income in a year, but still declared <u>bankruptcy</u> because of negative cash flow.

There are two primary reasons why net income (profit) and cash flow are not the same: The first is <u>depreciation</u> expense, a non-cash expense. Depreciation expense is an arbitrary method of spreading <u>capital</u> expenditures over time.

For example, if a firm pays $1 million for a piece of machinery, it may record depreciation expense of $100,000 in each of the next 10 years. That depreciation expense reduces net income, but it is not a cash expense in that year. The cash expenditure occurred when the firm paid $1 million for the machine.

The second reason is because there are differences between the date that a company actually buys or sells something and the date that it actually makes or receives payment. Think about when you bought something on credit. You had an expense when you charged the item to your credit card, but the actual cash flow may not have occurred for several weeks or months (but we don't recommend waiting months because you will be charged interest).

In a famous 1976 bankruptcy, the retail chain W.T. Grant *granted* (☺) credit to almost all its customers, many of whom did not pay their bills. Grant had positive accounting profits, but negative cash flow. Bankruptcy was inevitable.

THE LESSON

If you dread going to the mailbox, are receiving monthly overcharge fees from your bank, are using credit cards to pay off credit cards or praying for your next paycheck to come today, then you have a cash flow problem! Firms can manipulate and lie about their earnings (net income, accounting profit), but it is a lot harder to lie about cash flow. Firms want to collect cash as quickly as possible, but they also want to delay their payments for as long as possible. Just as companies must manage their cash flow, you have no choice but to do the same.

> *I'LL REPEAT SOMETHING YOU MIGHT*
> *CONSIDER TATOOING ON YOUR FOREHEAD;*
> *WHAT WE FEAR DOING MOST IS USUALLY*
> *WHAT WE MOST NEED TO DO.*
> — *Tim Ferriss*

Contrary to what most people believe, solving some of life's tough problems really is simple.

Want to lose weight? Eat less and exercise more; you will lose weight. Want to quit smoking? Stop buying cigarettes; nicotine problem solved. Addicted to that smartphone? Turn it off and put it away; problem solved.

Finally, if your personal finances are a case study in "cash flow disasters," then simply increase incoming revenue and decrease outgoing payments.

OK, you may be thinking, "Are these guys for real? Who are they kidding?"

We are for real and we are not kidding anybody.

Problems with weight, nicotine, smartphones, and personal finance are challenging millions of people every single day. And even though industries have been created to solve these debilitating problems, far too many people still fall short of their goals. We know it; we wrestle with some of these problems ourselves. We did not say the problems were *easy* to solve; we said the solutions were *simple* – you know what to do.

Overcoming your financial challenges is indeed simple; deep down in our souls, we know what to do. Tim Ferriss's quote captures the essence of this simplicity. The problem is not knowing what to do; the problem is having the courage, discipline, and dedication to do it. We fear the pain of changing what we need to do, even though we know we should do it.

If you are living paycheck to paycheck, falling further behind financially and emotionally, you have two choices: Continue that pattern or do what you fear doing; increase revenues and decrease costs. It is not easy, but it is simple. It also requires courage - the courage to take an honest look at yourself and your choices.

CENTRAL BANK

The Federal Reserve, also known as "the Fed," is the central bank of the United States. Throughout U.S. financial history, the idea of having a central bank has been controversial. Alexander Hamilton, one of its earliest supporters, squared off with Thomas Jefferson, who opposed it. Between 1791 and 1913, when our current Federal Reserve System was established, the United States had several periods when a central bank existed, and several when it did not.

Since 1913, the United States and every developed country in the world has created its own central bank. Foreign central banks include the ECB (European Central Bank), the BoE (Bank of England), BoJ (Bank of Japan) and the PBOC (People's Bank of China).

Central banks provide several services to their countries' economies and financial markets. The Fed, for instance, controls the money supply (monetary policy) to manage inflation, interest rates, unemployment and the stability of the economy, and the financial system. It also regulates banks and provides them with several services. As a lender of last resort to banks when they need money, the Fed, in essence, serves as a "bank for banks."

Since the Fed's creation, the United States has experienced 22 years of recession and one depression. In the 100 years prior to its creation, the nation experienced 44 years of recession, and six depressions. The Fed rescued the economy during the Great Recession from 2007 to 2009 and again during the 2020 coronavirus panic.

THE LESSON

Tracking the Fed's interest rate decisions makes you a smart decision maker for your personal finances. "Don't fight the Fed" is a Wall Street adage that advises investors to buy stocks when the Fed lowers interest rates. Also, whenever you use banking services, realize that your bank is part of a larger, Fed-regulated system. The interest rates on your car loans, mortgages, business loans, CDs, and credit cards are all affected by the Fed's actions. The value of your investment portfolio is also affected by interest rates that the Fed sets and influences. You may do your banking on Main Street, but your bank is just around the corner from Washington, D.C.

> ## *UNLESS YOU ARE WILLING TO COMPROMISE, SOCIETY CANNOT LIVE TOGETHER.*
> ## *— Alan Greenspan*

Alan Greenspan chaired the Federal Reserve from 1987 to 2006, serving under four Presidents: Reagan, George H.W. Bush, Clinton and George W. Bush. His style, and performance during this period resulted in his fans, the press and even some of his critics referring to him as "The Maestro."

Greenspan and all Fed chairs before and after him were responsible for balancing competing economic forces: inflation, interest rates, job growth, consumer prices. Decisions on lowering, raising or holding the line on interest rates were based on a fundamental philosophical and pragmatic approach: compromise. Bottom line: the Fed balances inflationary forces in the context of employment trends and the economy.

The very essence of our message to you is based on the same mission driven approach of the Fed: Your *total wealth*, financial security and personal fulfillment are the result of compromises you make daily. These compromises reflect the reality that life challenges us with a series of never-ending, and often conflicting choices.

We either balance the short-term and long-term gains and losses of our choices, or we pay the consequences. We must balance our financial goals with family goals, and pay the consequences of those choices.

Earlier, we quoted Dale Carnegie: "Success is getting what you want; happiness is wanting what you get." Your journey through life should not be a trade-off between success and happiness. It should be a compromise, resulting in a joyous fusion of success *and* happiness.

A maestro is one who leads, controls and creates while engendering respect from others who marvel at his or her performance. Be the maestro in your own life and over your personal finances. Create balance and harmony through compromise.

THE SEC

The U.S. Securities and Exchange Commission (SEC) was created in 1934 during the Great Depression. Its missions were, and still are, "to protect investors, maintain fair, orderly and efficient markets, and facilitate capital formation."

The SEC requires publicly traded companies to provide accurate information about themselves, and to fairly release that information so that all investors can receive it at the same time.

It regulates securities markets and exchanges such as the NYSE and NASDAQ, securities firms, brokers, investment advisors, bond (credit) ratings agencies, mutual funds and ETFs.

All new rules and rule changes undergo a "benefit-cost" analysis; if a new rule protects you as an investor (a benefit), it will likely create a burden on companies, exchanges or financial advisors (a cost).

Working with the Financial Accounting Standards Board (FASB) and the Public Company Accounting Oversight Board (PCAOB), the SEC enforces securities laws. It oversees accountants and auditors. It also works with similar international agencies and state regulators.

Typical cases that require the SEC to investigate include misleading or omitted information about a security, market manipulation, theft of securities or money, improper treatment of investors by brokers, securities firms and/or financial advisors, fraud and insider trading.

THE LESSON

You may be dealing with a financial advisor, an accountant or a broker. All of those agents are regulated by the SEC, and you should be glad they are. You may buy stocks, bonds, mutual funds and ETFs. All of these securities are monitored by the SEC. You are being protected in an arena where financial transactions necessarily require oversight and regulation. You are a taxpayer; the SEC is on your payroll. If you want confirmation of where your dollars are being spent, go to their website, sec.gov. Click on the EDUCATION tab. ♪

> *PROTECTION AND SECURITY ARE ONLY VALUABLE IF THEY DO NOT CRAMP LIFE EXCESSIVELY.*
> *— Carl Jung*

We bet you have never met anyone who received a speeding ticket and was happy to get it. We are also pretty sure that if *you* ever received a speeding ticket, you weren't too thrilled either.

But we are also willing to wager that you support traffic laws and are glad to have police and traffic courts that enforce them – keeping the streets safe.

People have a certain ambivalence towards rules, regulations and the sanctions for violating them. Intuitively, we accept that safety, security, and protection are important. After all, there are bad people out there and we should be protected from them. We should also be protected from dangerous situations.

But when those sanctions apply to us, we often sing a different tune. Now those rules are oppressive, infringe on our freedom and, to quote Jung, "cramp life excessively."

Our ambivalence about rules and protection is also reflected in whether we are being protected, or whether we are the protectors. When you are imposing rules and regulations on your children living at home, you feel fully justified in doing so. After all, it's your home, and you believe the rules are best for everyone living there.

Your children however, especially if they are in their teens or beyond, are most likely feeling excessively cramped, and possibly question why they can't be trusted to do the right thing.

Bottom line on rules, regulations, and sanctions:

If it is a law, obey it.
If you break it, pay the consequences.
If you impose rules, expect pushback.

Don't make yourself crazy. You can't have it both ways. You can't have protection and security and total freedom. If you want security, you must also pay the price of feeling a little "cramped."

It is what it is!

STOCK EXCHANGES

A stock exchange is a market where shares of stock are traded. Bonds, options and futures contracts also trade on exchanges. Today, there are more than 50 stock exchanges operating around the world.

The New York Stock Exchange (NYSE) is the largest exchange in the world. In April 2020, it boasted a total market value (market cap) of stocks trading at over $25 trillion.

Not far behind is The National Association of Securities Dealers Automatic Quotations, better known by its acronym, NASDAQ, which had a market value of approximately $11 trillion for the same period.

In its own claim to fame, the NASDAQ has become the electronic marketplace of competing "market makers," who quote bid prices, at which they will buy shares, and asked prices, at which they will sell them.

Asked prices are always higher than bid prices, allowing these market makers to profit on the bid-asked "spread." For example, they may be willing to buy a stock for $40 per share and sell the same stock for $40.05 per share; the spread is a nickel.

On a typical day, several billion shares of stock trade on the NYSE and NASDAQ; this figure is known as "volume." The corporations that first issued those shares had nothing to do with the trades, each of which had an individual buyer and seller; they were just trades between investors.

Stock exchange trading is known as the "secondary market." When a company first sells its shares to the public, it does so in an initial public offering (IPO). When companies sell their shares to the public, they do so in the "primary market." Primary market transactions are relatively uncommon, but the secondary market is huge.

THE LESSON

Stock exchanges provide liquidity, allowing you to easily buy and sell shares in corporations. Stock exchanges also make it easier for corporations to raise capital, allowing them to grow and create jobs and wealth. In general, you should not care if you trade stocks listed on the NYSE or NASDAQ. However, so-called OTC (over the counter) "pink sheet" stocks are generally very speculative. Also known as "penny stocks," (their price is usually less than a dollar), the stocks are less regulated than others, have less liquidity and provide less information about their corporate performance.

Stock exchanges are places where securities ... shares of stock, bonds, options and futures contracts ... are traded. Flea markets are places where almost anything smaller than a bulldozer is traded, and sometimes even the bulldozer itself.

The former markets are characterized by knowledgeable market makers executing buy-and-sell decisions on the fly. The latter markets are characterized by people who look like they stepped out of a Norman Rockwell painting, selling something they made or collected, and deciding on a sale price while looking you in the eye.

Stock exchanges are venues for trades that enable traders to create and/or manage wealth. Those exchanges exist for the sole purpose of buyers and sellers making financial trades. Flea markets are venues for creating friends and a memorable purchase. Stock exchanges are about money; flea markets are about heart and soul.

Yet there are times when stock exchanges also reflect heart and soul.

Stocks or bonds that have been held in a family for decades, called "family bonds" or "family stocks," have significance beyond their monetary value. They mean something special to a family emotionally, not just monetarily. Yes, corporate or municipal bonds can bond a family.

These stocks and bonds, like handmade trinkets at a flea market, have stories behind them. When a family member trades one of these stocks or bonds, the story often ends with a tinge of regret, regardless of the profits the seller realizes.

When that happens, a stock exchange is like a flea market. The seller is parting with a family keepsake.

INFLATION AND DEFLATION

Inflation occurs when prices increase. Put another way, the value of the currency declines. So, if the price of an apple rises from 25 cents to 50 cents, we have inflation, as the value of a dollar declines from four apples to two. Inflation "debases" a currency; the dollar buys less.

Deflation occurs when the prices of goods and services decline.

Unexpectedly high inflation and deflation both create problems. Thus, in recent years, the Federal Reserve has been trying to keep inflation steady at about 2 percent per year.

Measuring inflation is difficult. Exactly what goods and services should be measured? We all consume different things, and the quality of those goods and services changes over time. If a car has more standard and safety features added, the price will rise. Is the price increase because of inflation or those added features?

Nonetheless, several indexes measure inflation. The Consumer Price Index (CPI) measures changes in the prices of a basket of goods and services purchased by an average urban consumer. The Producer Price Index (PPI) measures price changes in the selling prices of goods and services from the manufacturer's perspective; it measures the cost of production at the wholesale level. The GDP deflator is a broad measure of prices of all domestically produced goods and services in the United States. Unlike the basket of goods behind the CPI, the goods and services underlying the GDP deflator changes from one year to the next.

THE LESSON

Extremely high inflation and any amount of deflation are two of the most worrisome risks you face as an investor; either could derail your financial planning. Savings accounts are especially vulnerable to inflation if the inflation rate exceeds the account's interest rate. Savings accounts are also vulnerable to deflation because the interest rates they offer are lower when there is deflation. Your social security payments may increase if the CPI increases. Cost of living wage adjustments (raises) and other fees may also depend on the CPI. The rates of return offered by Treasury Inflation Protected Securities (TIPS), a type of U.S. government treasury bond, rise and fall with changes in the CPI. Monitor inflation indices and adjust your financial plan accordingly.

> ## IF YOU WANT A GUARANTEE BUY A TOASTER.
> ## — Clint Eastwood

Undoubtedly, you have heard someone say, "The only sure things in life are death and taxes." Possibly, someone heard you say it. Whether motivated by cynicism or realism, this observation about life emphasizes the uncertainty and unpredictability about our tomorrows.

The purchasing power of your dollar tomorrow, next month and next year is not guaranteed, and never will be (except in a country with total price controls; let's hope that never happens).

So, how do you live in a world with no guarantees, without going crazy and without making other people crazy?

You maintain your physical health. Uncertainty and chaos will test your resilience and ability to rebound. Without physical stamina, a healthy diet and regular exercise, the uncertainty and chaos will beat you down.

You avoid dangerous drugs and excessive alcohol. A predictable response to pain, be it emotional or physical is to deaden it. Drugs and alcohol serve that purpose, but they come with too great a cost – a debilitating cost.

You accept the reality of uncertainty and reframe it as an opportunity. Yes, you can turn lemons into lemonade; you can also be a franchisor of lemonade stands.

You reach out to family and friends when you need support; you can also provide support when they need it. They too are trying to cope in a world without guarantees.

You accept the basic premise of this book, a premise based on the yin-and-yang forces of life. As we stated in the Introduction, the yin and the yang connote the complementary, harmonious fusion of seemingly opposite forces. You accept that both financial wealth, and psychological and physical health, represent attainable goals and outcomes, even in times of uncertainty.

Because life is uncertain and unpredictable you have the opportunity (and it is an opportunity) to experience the challenge and the power of personal achievement.

We guarantee it!

RECESSION

Economies are often characterized as either being in expansion or recession. In the United States, the National Bureau of Economic Research (NBER) makes the call between those alternatives. In a recession, the gross domestic product (GDP), which measures the value of all goods and services produced by the U.S. economy during a period of time, declines. Recessions also trigger job losses across the economy.

The NBER declares the beginning and ending dates of recessions with a lag. For instance, the NBER declared in December 2008 that a recession had begun in December 2007. This means that a recession could be beginning as you read this, but you won't officially know it for several months – maybe a year or more. Between 1970 and 2015, the U.S. economy was in recession 15 percent of the time.

Stocks are a leading indicator of recessions; they typically decline before a recession begins and begin recovering before it ends. It would be great if you could predict recessions so that you could sell your stocks in advance. But don't bother trying and don't believe anyone who says he can. Economic forecasting of recessions is very poor; some make a lucky prediction, but no one is consistently accurate.

THE LESSON

Two Lessons:

If you are more than 10 years from retirement, have a strong stomach and are experiencing a recession, we recommend you bet that things will reverse. Recessions have always reversed, in the U.S. So, when things are at their darkest – the stock market plummets by 30 to 40 percent – take a deep breath, take a chance and be a contrarian. Increase your asset allocation to stocks. Invest in stock mutual funds and ETFs with low expense ratios (strongly consider buying index funds). Be optimistic that the economy will recover.

We advocate for a target stock/bond asset allocation appropriate for your age and degree of risk aversion. If there is a recession, and the stock market has declined, you may now be below your target in stocks. Consult with your advisor before rebalancing. You don't want to jeopardize your retirement by taking on excessive risk given the uncertainty and your retirement goals.

You will have good days and bad days in life. There will be times when you will feel like climbing a mountain, and times when you won't even want to get out of bed. There will be moments when you are just going through the motions, functioning at 50 percent, and moments when you feel turbocharged.

We will experience peaks. But peaks exist only because of valleys, which we also will experience.

Because of changes in our physical and psychological health, and because of increasing and decreasing stresses in our life, we will periodically experience slumps. But here's the good news: They are not permanent.

Just as economic recessions are cyclical and temporary, so too are our personal slumps. To ensure your slumps are temporary follow these five simple rules:

1. Expect the slump to be temporary. Believing and expecting otherwise will turn a bad day into a regrettable life.

2. Examine and correct any self-defeating behaviors that might be causing the slump. If you don't change, and external pressures don't change, the slump doesn't change.

3. Seek advice and counsel from others. Friends and families may notice your self-defeating behaviors but may be reluctant to offer help because they don't want to hurt you. That is why you should solicit it, and be grateful when it's offered.

4. Stop scapegoating. Blaming people or other pressures for your slump will not change things; it only makes you bitter.

5. Keep swinging.

We believe Hank Aaron built his professional career following these simple rules. After all, on April 8, 1974, he hit his 715th home run, breaking Babe Ruth's Major League record.

TIME VALUE OF MONEY

Would you rather have $1 million dollars today or $1 million five years from today?

Almost surely we all would say "today." We would choose the money now without hesitation, almost reflexively. Why is that so?

The answer is simple: Money in hand today is worth more than that same amount at some time in the future. This differential value of the same amount of money today versus tomorrow defines the time value of money. Aside from the psychological benefit of immediate versus deferred gratification, there are two financial explanations for the time value of money: inflation and investment opportunity.

First, inflation. How many times have you heard someone say: "I remember the good old days when things weren't so expensive"? If only you could have $10 every time you did; you would not need this book to increase your wealth.

It's true, your money *did* buy more in the "good old days." The purchasing power of $10 today is less than it was 10 years ago, and greater than it will be 10 years in the future. Blame inflation. To quote Yogi Berra, *"A nickel ain't worth a dime anymore."*

Now, lost investment opportunity. Time allows today's dollars to increase in value if those dollars are invested at the competitive and prevailing interest rate and that interest compounds over time. Indeed, money has the potential to earn money, but that potential depends on your decision to make money work for you by leveraging the passage of time. How much will X dollars be worth in the future? Formulas at the back of this book answer that question.

THE LESSON

You now have another interpretation for the axiom "time is money," and this interpretation goes well beyond counting minutes and hours, or monitoring the labor purchased during those hours. Inflation and lost opportunities are silent thieves, stealing from your account. So, if you have a choice between taking the same amount of money now or later, take it now and thank your good fortune later. Plan for the future but live for today. ♪

"Always in the now." With that four-word mantra, Willie Nelson, the great country sage, has distilled the complexity of life, bringing heart and soul to the concept of time value of money – one of the most important concepts guiding financial planning.

But don't be fooled into believing that by focusing on now, Willie is calling for hedonism or gratification at the expense of others. And don't assume that analyzing time, interest rates and economic forces is necessarily an exercise in personal greed.

To the contrary, "always in the now" is a potential life-altering perspective that forces us to focus on *now* – the only temporal span we can control, and the only minutes, seconds, and hours we can directly impact.

Can you change *the* future? No. Can you change *your* future? Of course you can...by making the right decisions now.

Because time is finite (we will all die) and irreplaceable, how and why you spend it will define the quality of your life. As philosophers have told us for centuries, and as self-help gurus continually tell us, yesterday can never be retrieved or done over; and tomorrow is simply a dream, a hope, a vision.

What was was, and what will be will be. You are always in the now and only in the now. Appreciate the current moment, for it is indeed priceless, and ultimately a gift not given to everyone.

COMPOUND INTEREST

Compound interest is, quite simply, the result of interest earning interest. Consider an example:

You invest $100 in a savings account that pays 10 percent interest per year (10% is called the interest rate; it is the price you receive for lending money). If interest is *not* compounded (called "simple interest"), then you earn $10/year; after two years, you have $120. If interest is compounded, then in the second year, your initial $10 of interest also earns 10 percent interest, so you after two years you have $121. That extra dollar is the result of your interest earning interest; it is the result of compound interest.

One extra dollar doesn't sound like much, but over long periods of time, the impact of compounding is more impressive. Suppose you invest that $100 for 50 years. After 50 years of simple interest, you will earn $10/year x 50 years = $500 in simple interest, and you will have a total of $600. But with 50 years of compound interest, your investment will be worth $11,739. With compound interest, your interest earns an additional $11,139, compared to simple interest!

Your interest can compound more frequently than yearly, which helps even more. Suppose that you invest your $100 to earn 10 percent interest, compounded monthly (instead of annually). After 50 years, your investment will be worth $14,537!

The "Rule of 72" is a nifty approximation and application of compound interest. It states that the product of your <u>rate of return</u> times the number of years it takes to double your investment equals 72. How long will it take you to double your money if you earn 6%? The Rule of 72 says: about 12 years (6×12=72); the actual number of years is 11.90.

THE LESSON

Einstein supposedly said, *"Compound interest is the eighth wonder of the world."* Start investing early and let your interest compound as frequently as possible and at the highest rate possible. Be patient. You are building your <u>wealth</u> over the long haul; think years and decades, not days and months. There are high earners who retire with modest portfolios and moderate earners who retire with rich portfolios. The latter were patient, frugal and understood that interest compounded over time is indeed the eighth wonder of world. <u>Leverage</u> that wonder. ♪

> *HABITS ARE THE COMPOUND*
> *INTEREST OF SELF-IMPROVEMENT.*
> *— James Clear*

The essence of compounding is easily understood. By steadily adding to an activity over time, you are accelerating the growth, or development of that activity. If the activity is investing, compounding increases the growth of that investment, often resulting in a happily unexpected outcome.

Because compounding has multiple applications, we have a powerful explanation for why some of us seem to get happier, healthier and personally fulfilled over time while others regress into physical and spiritual decay. Those who grow and flourish develop positive behaviors that compound over time. Those who regress develop negative behaviors compounded over time.

Compounding thus has two possible paths: ever expanding upward or ever contracting downward. In both cases, the driving force is the behavior you choose – positive or negative.

Our choices over time will inevitably and inexorably define the quality of our life and the legacy we leave behind. Achieving the good things in life is indeed possible and predictable given the power of compounding. But so is loss and decay.

If you understand the cumulative power of behaviors, compounding, and time, you will stop searching for the secret of eternal happiness. Because of this trilogy, you also will realize that we have the power to make our own luck. As someone once said, "Success is a matter of luck, ask any failure."

Of course life is unpredictable and randomly fortunate or unfortunate. But your misfortune need not be compounded; change your behavior and you change your luck.

RATE OF RETURN

A rate of return measures how much money you make on an investment during a holding period. It is a percentage return on your initial investment.

The money you make comes from two sources: a periodic <u>cash flow</u> paid by the <u>asset</u> (coupon interest for a <u>bond</u> or <u>dividends</u> for a <u>stock</u>), and <u>capital gain</u>s or losses (price increases or price decreases). If you have capital losses, it means the value of your investment declined and your rate of return may be negative.

For example, if you buy one share of stock for $100, and at the end of your holding period the share is worth $105, your capital gain is $5, and your rate of return is 5 percent.

Typically, this simple definition for rate of return is used when the holding period is short: a year or less. For longer periods, and/or when you have bought and sold shares more than once, the computation of the rate of return is more complicated.

THE LESSON

The rate of return is a measure of investment performance. When there is one cash flow (e.g., one dividend), no trading cash flows other than an initial purchase and a final sale, and when the holding period is short, the rate of return is a simple calculation. But for long periods, and/or when you have made multiple purchases and sales or received several dividends, computing a rate of return can be complex. It is important that your advisor, if you use one, adheres to accurate methods of measuring performance. Make sure she uses reliable data and understands the limitations of the methods. ♪

Emily Post, who died in 1960, was the iconic arbiter of etiquette. Not only was she the go-to authority on social graces, but she also established a brand that produces advice books to this very day.

You are undoubtedly wondering why we chose a quote from a mid-20th century etiquette guru for a perspective on rate of return. After all, she is not talking about finances, and her advice predates virtual meetings, social media, and email.

We chose her quote because of a common complaint in letters to advice columnists. You may have read some and even thought that one or two hit home.

Here are a few paraphrases from those letters:

Why aren't (children/grandchildren/friends/newly married couples) thanking me for the gift I sent?
Signed: Sad and Heart Broken

Why don't invited guests have the courtesy to respond to an RSVP?
Signed: Frustrated Beyond Belief

Get the picture? Sad and Frustrated are telling the world that an investment of time, money and effort devoted to gifting and planning deserve an acknowledgment, a return on that investment. They are *emotionally invested*, expecting the courtesy of a response.

Is expecting a thank you note or a commitment to attend or not attend outdated or unreasonable? We don't think so. Courtesy is never outdated.

The heart and soul of receiving a gift or a request to RSVP is acknowledging the kindness by responding in kind.

Consider this: If Emily Post's advice is outdated, why do gift shops, bookstores and card shops still sell thank you cards? Some of those cards are even blank, allowing for a truly personal response. A handwritten thank you note will be remembered and appreciated for a long time.

But if you prefer to send an eCard, we think Emily would still approve.

BEHAVIORAL FINANCE

You are not as rational in your buy-sell decisions as you think!

Because of cognitive biases, we often make buy-sell decisions that are not only irrational, but often self-destructive. For example, different types of <u>stocks</u> exhibit <u>rate-of-return</u> patterns that cannot be explained by a simple <u>risk</u>-return tradeoff. Likewise, many investors make the same types of biased trading errors, causing them to underperform, and lose money.

Researchers have found that even after adjusting for risk differences, small cap stocks tend to outperform large cap stocks; value stocks tend to outperform growth stocks; and stocks that have performed well during the past 3-12 months outperform recent losers. All three of these patterns have been explained, at least in part, by investor trading habits and biases – what we call behavioral finance.

Consider these findings:

When individual investors sell one stock and then buy another shortly thereafter, the stock sold usually outperforms the one purchased!

You may hold on to losers too long and sell winners too soon. Holding losers is consistent with something called loss aversion. You are loss averse if losing $1,000 causes you more pain than the pleasure of making a $1000 profit.

Overconfidence and herd mentality bias your trades. If you think you are a better-than-average investor, smarter than the next guy, or "know" a stock is about to rise or fall, then you are an overconfident investor. Herd mentality means joining the crowd in panic buying or selling, resulting in bubbles and crashes.

THE LESSON

Study your trading habits. Are you exhibiting any of the above behavioral traits? Are you inadvertently buying high and selling low? Monitor your performance. If you are underperforming relative to a broadly diversified <u>market index</u>, either change the basis for your trading decisions or just buy and hold <u>index funds</u>. Stock performance is random; cognitive biases are predictable. Your biases are also predictable...if you study them and if you acknowledge them.

> *IT'S NICE TO HAVE A LOT OF MONEY, BUT YOU KNOW, YOU DON'T WANT TO KEEP IT AROUND FOREVER. I PREFER BUYING THINGS. OTHERWISE, IT'S A LITTLE LIKE SAVING SEX FOR YOUR OLD AGE.*
> — Warren Buffett

Warren Buffett's lighthearted observation speaks to the essence of behavioral finance. "Saving sex for your old age" is indeed a savings plan likely to result in little if any yield. It is also a savings plan you would be crazy to carry out.

Periodically, we hear or read stories about someone who worked in jobs that provided income – not wealth – and lived a meager lifestyle, a poster child for frugality. Upon his death, our poster child bequeathed a multi million dollar estate to an organization or cause for which he had a lifelong passion.

When you read or hear stories like these, do you think that person was crazy? Regardless of your assessment, chances are the person found his life personally rewarding. He did exactly what he wanted to do.

You too will manage your money the way you want to, depending on your deep-seated feelings about money...what it's for, and how it should be used. For example, believing that "money is the root of all evil" or that "money is bestowed upon the worthy" will directly affect how you earn, spend, invest, and bequeath it.

Our self-image will also affect how we manage money. We all have feelings of self-esteem (positive, negative, mixed), and a sense of worthiness. The combination of these feelings and beliefs help you understand the power and implication of behavioral finance, and why your money management may be self-defeating.

Finally, don't assume that because of state-of-the-art software and hardware, top decision makers in large corporations are immune from biases. To the contrary, coaching top executives to control their decision-making biases is a growth industry.

Artificial intelligence may generate data and provide decision makers with best case - worst case scenarios, but the toughest decisions are always made by human beings. You are human; understand your biases. We all have them.

AGENCY PROBLEM

Have you ever asked or expected someone to do something on your behalf?

This describes a principal-agent relationship. If you expect someone else to make decisions for you, you are the principal and the other party is the agent. But agency relationships create a dilemma: You don't know if the agent will make decisions to benefit *you* or themselves.

There is often a conflict of interest, and this conflict is called the agency problem

Unfortunately, <u>finance</u> is replete with agency problems. If you are a stockholder, you expect the corporation's management (the agent) to make decisions in your best interest and increase the value of its common <u>stock</u>...and your <u>wealth</u>. However, corporate management can also make decisions to benefit themselves, not the stockholders.

Another agency problem arises when you hire a wealth advisor (the agent) to manage your wealth.   Will your wealth manager make decisions to increase your wealth or theirs?

Historically, some wealth advisors have exploited their clients. For example, prior to 1975, when investors paid high commissions to trade stocks, unscrupulous money managers would churn their clients' accounts, meaning that they over-traded stocks for their clients, generating high commissions for themselves in the process. A 1940 book written by Fred Schwed, Jr. asked "Where are the Customer's Yachts?" The bankers and brokers had them, but not the customers.

Another agency problem occurs when wealth managers put investors in poorly performing <u>alternative investments</u> (e.g., hedge funds) that charge high fees.

THE LESSON

The agency problem is a reason that the financial services industry and securities markets are highly regulated by the <u>Securities and Exchange Commission (SEC)</u>, the Financial Industry Regulatory Authority (FINRA), and the Consumer Financial Protection Bureau (CFPB). Always be aware of possible conflicts of interest when another party is acting on your behalf, especially concerning your money. If the management of a corporation of which you own shares is overcompensated while the stock price is underperforming, consider selling those shares.

> *IF I WAS BEING PAID $30,000 A YEAR,*
> *THE VERY LEAST I COULD DO WAS HIT .400.*
> — *Ted Williams*

Google the phrase "Hire the right person." At the time of this writing, that phrase yielded 9.7 million hits. A random scan of some of those hits takes you to books, articles, consultants, TED talks, testing services, employment agencies, YouTube lectures, self-assessments, and attorneys. The last item speaks to the potential risks of hiring someone who you now wish had been hired by your competitor.

The common theme across those 9.7 million hits? Even though hiring the right person is one of the most important decisions any company will make, it is a decision fraught with potentially significant costs – financial and human.

Without a doubt, the hiring decision is as much art as it is science. The right decision will increase your productivity and yield untold benefits. The wrong decision will create sleepless nights, lost productivity and possible sessions with an attorney.

The person you hire represents you and your company. That person is, in a very real sense, your agent, hired to act on your behalf, increase your wealth, your company's value and to do so ethically and legally.

Once your agent starts believing and acting as if you work for him, and not vice versa, it's time to say "goodbye and good luck." It's also time to ask yourself basic questions: Why did you hire this person? What should you have done differently to prevent what you thought was a good decision from going bad? What did the agent see in you that enabled him to do what he did? Answer those questions, and you will live, learn and prosper.

Super stars like Ted Williams are rare and always will be. But that doesn't mean you should stop looking for them, or that you believe you can't become one.

Indeed, if you are someone else's agent, work to become that person's star!

CAPITAL 101

"Capital" is one of the most multi-functional and important words in the world of finance. Here, are its most common usages:

- *Capitalism* is an economic system in which companies and individuals privately own the means of production. In socialism, the government owns the plant, property and equipment. A *capitalist* is an individual who invests in companies and their assets to earn profits.
- *Physical capital* is a tangible asset, consisting of plant, property and equipment. A *capital-intensive* company uses more plant and equipment and less labor. *Capital budgeting* evaluates whether a financial investment in physical capital is worthwhile. If it is, the firm makes *capital expenditures*.
- *Financial capital* is used to acquire physical capital. Companies either borrow (debt, bonds) to buy plant, property and equipment, or use owners' money (equity) to buy it. The stock and bonds a corporation issues are financial capital.
- When firms decide the mix of debt and equity to issue to finance their operations, it is called the capital structure decision.
- *Capital gains* and *capital losses* are realized when the prices of your investments rise (for gains) or fall (for losses).
- *Working capital*, assets likely to be converted to cash within a year, consists of cash, short-term marketable securities such as treasury bills, accounts receivable (customers that still owe for products purchased) and inventory that will be converted into a finished product and sold within a year. The difference between current assets and current liabilities is called *net working capital*.
- *Human capital* is the value of your skills, talents and knowledge.
- *Market capitalization* ("*market cap*") is the value of a firm's common stock, computed as the stock price times the number of shares outstanding.
- Companies are *capitalized* when they issue shares of common stock and/or bonds. You may *capitalize* on an opportunity by using it to your advantage.
- *Venture capital* describes investing in the stock of a startup company.

THE LESSON

The examples above will help you understand common corporate financial jargon. Unless you are employed in a large company, you may never use these phrases. But if someone tosses around these terms, they will no longer intimidate you. Knowledge is power. You have just increased your intellectual capital; keep it up.

> *IF YOU'RE ONE IN A MILLION IN CHINA*
> *THERE'S STILL 1,300 PEOPLE JUST LIKE YOU.*
> — *Thomas Friedman*

In 2005, Thomas Friedman wrote a worldwide best seller, *The World is Flat: A Brief History of the 21st Century*. His observations and predictions about geo-political, technological and economic forces have since been studied and quoted in college classrooms, corporate boardrooms and even the halls of Congress.

His thesis, which serves as the flattened world metaphor, is that global competition for resources, talent and venture capital is playing out on a level playing field. Technology and human capital are driving forces behind that leveling.

Friedman's quote captures the essence of the human dimension in a flattened world. Financial and physical capital will always be important, but a flattened world makes them secondary to intellectual capital. You may be the smartest, most innovative and energetic person wherever you work, but your competition is not in your company. It is anyone in the world with access to hardware, software and broadband.

Once you fully grasp that Google provides information access to anyone, anywhere at any time, you understand why the world is flat. In this increasingly flattened world, your most important capital is intellectual capital: what you know, how you apply it, and how you work with others.

The good news is your intellectual capital is potentially infinite and renewable. The only constraints are those you impose. Intellectual capital: Say it three times, internalize it and accept it as your personal mantra as you move forward in this increasingly flattened world.

EFFICIENCY

Efficiency is a key financial concept with multiple meanings. The most important one relates to the "efficient markets hypothesis," which means that prices reflect known information.

When news breaks about a company – its latest product is selling like hotcakes, the CEO has just been fired, etc. – its <u>stock</u> price quickly changes to reflect that news. You may get a higher or lower <u>rate of return</u> than what you expected when you first bought the stock because the news was unexpected.

If markets are efficient, you always get a fair deal when you buy a <u>stock</u>, priced to provide you with a fair, <u>risk</u>-adjusted <u>expected rate of return</u>, based on known information. Investors who buy or sell *after* they hear announcements should not expect to make unusually high rates of return.

There are several other meanings of efficiency:

An "efficient portfolio" offers the highest expected rate of return, given its risk. For every level of risk there is a different efficient portfolio. The greater the risk, the greater is the portfolio's expected rate of return.

"Efficiency ratios" measure how firms manage their <u>assets</u> to generate sales and profits.

When investment <u>capital</u> and labor flow to the most deserving companies, products and projects, we are referring to "allocational efficiency"; well-managed companies and their best projects receive the funds they need to operate and succeed.

Finally, because of <u>behavioral finance</u>, markets may not be as efficient as we once believed. Investors' biases and trading errors may lead to mispriced stocks; identifying which ones are mispriced is difficult.

THE LESSON

Two lessons:

First, market prices reflect public information, not private inside information. Insider trading, when individuals trade on important private information, is a crime.

Second, because markets are quite efficient, actively managed <u>mutual funds</u> rarely overcome the handicap of their expenses and hence, rarely outperform low-cost <u>index funds</u>. When you invest in stocks, seriously consider investing most or all of your money in index funds with very low expense ratios. ♪

> *MAKE SPACE IN YOUR LIFE FOR THE THINGS THAT MATTER, FOR FAMILY AND FRIENDS, LOVE AND GENEROSITY, FUN AND JOY. WITHOUT THIS, YOU WILL BURN OUT IN MID-CAREER AND WONDER WHERE YOUR LIFE WENT.*
> — Jonathan Sacks

Ultimately, this quote reinforces the potential tragedy of acquiring riches while losing family and friends. You have undoubtedly read or heard advice similar to this quote. Almost all self-help books offer variations of this advice for achieving personal fulfillment.

You probably also accept its emotional power for changing lives. Any reasonable person hoping to have a fulfilling life knows the advice makes sense. The problem is creating a life where that wisdom becomes a reality, so that you don't have to "wonder where your life went."

The issue is not whether you love your family and friends. The issue is are you *there* for your family and friends? Did you "make space" for them?

The good news is there is a solution to the problem: applying the logic and implications of efficiency. "Making space in your life" ultimately comes down to the decisions you make about how you will spend your time.

There are only 60 minutes in an hour, 24 hours in a day. Allocating this precious resource across multiple and often conflicting priorities means deciding what to do when, and that decision is the essence of efficiency. Yes, efficiency has heart-and-soul implications.

Finally, when you get a chance, listen to Harry Chapin's recording of "Cat's in the Cradle." Our life is a series of decisions and consequences, not wishes and consequences. If you want to change consequences, change your decisions, then think about the most efficient way to implement those decisions.

LIQUIDITY

Financial liquidity describes the ability to buy or sell something quickly at a fair price. An illiquid <u>asset</u> cannot be so easily sold. For example, real estate is typically an illiquid asset. You may have to wait months to get the price you want.

There are three components to the liquidity of securities in general, and <u>stocks</u> specifically:

The first is the bid-ask spread. The bid price (always lower than the asked price) is the price you get for selling the stock. The asked price is what you pay for the stock. Very liquid stocks may have bid-asked spreads of only a penny or two. Less liquid stocks have wider spreads, sometimes several dollars.

The second is the number of shares you can trade at the bid and asked <u>quotes</u>. You can buy or sell many shares (perhaps thousands) at the quoted bid and asked prices of a liquid stock. But you may only be able to trade 100 shares at the quotes of an illiquid stock.

The third is price pressure. Suppose only 100 shares are being offered at the asked price. How much more will you have to pay if you want to buy more shares? A penny or two more per share might define a liquid stock. It might cost you a dollar or two more per share to buy more shares of an illiquid stock. This aspect of liquidity is called "market depth." When a market is deep, you can trade large volumes of stock with little impact on its price. The market for illiquid stocks is said to be "thin."

Many experts believe that illiquid stocks sell at discounted prices to compensate for their illiquidity.

THE LESSON

Invest some of your portfolio in safe, liquid investments such as savings accounts, bank CD's and money market <u>mutual funds</u>. You may wish to have three to six months of living expenses in these types of investments. If you own a company, keep enough current assets (cash and safe short-term securities) to improve your liquidity. When money is scarce, the Federal Reserve injects liquidity into the financial system so financial assets can be sold at fair prices.

> *ONE OF THE MOST FREQUENLY MENTIONED DIMENSIONS OF THE FLOW EXPERIENCE IS THAT, WHILE IT LASTS, ONE IS ABLE TO FORGET ALL THE UNPLEASANT ASPECTS OF LIFE.*
> — Mihaly Csikszentmihalyi

Financial liquidity is all about flow: some assets flow between buyer and seller quicker than others.

The concept of flow also applies to human behavior and was the title of Csikszentmihalyi's best-selling book *Flow: The Psychology of Optimal Experience*. His thesis – a state of effortless concentration – has profound impact as we search for meaning and fulfillment in our lives. We achieve our fullest potential and are happiest, whether at play or at work, when we experience flow.

When you are concentrating and focusing, but not thinking about concentrating or focusing, you are experiencing flow... an optimal experience.

Athletes often refer to periods in their life when they were in the zone. During those times, they felt their athletic prowess was at a peak and were able to perform at an almost superhuman level.

Anyone reading this book has experienced flow or longs to experience it. If you have ever been totally involved in a task, shutting out all distractions, you were experiencing flow. If you ever felt an energized focus and a heightened motivation, you were experiencing flow. If you ever felt total enjoyment in simply performing a task, you were experiencing flow.

Imagine getting high psychologically and emotionally without ever popping a pill. Flow doesn't come from drugs; you must totally immerse yourself in whatever you are doing to experience it.

If you can imagine it, you can do it, and when you do it you are in the flow -- reaping the benefit of a type of wealth available to anyone.

We wish you the priceless joy of flow on your journey towards achieving your *total wealth*.

OPPORTUNITY COST

Opportunity cost is an economic concept; it is the second-best choice, compared to the decision you make. Every decision you make comes with an opportunity cost because you always could have made a different decision.

If you order a hamburger for dinner, an opportunity cost is the pizza you could have chosen instead. If you buy a new pair of shoes, an opportunity cost might be that you could have paid down your credit card debt.

If you decide to invest in a particular stock, the opportunity cost is the other stock that you could have purchased; more accurately, it is the difference between the returns of the two stocks.

Everything you own has an opportunity cost, because you always could sell your assets; the potential selling price is the opportunity cost of ownership.

Corporations face a cost of the financial capital they need. They raise equity and debt to invest in property, equipment, and businesses. The investors who provide the capital have their opportunity cost, which is the rate of return they believe they could earn if they didn't buy the company's securities. There are many other investments, with similar risks, they could have made.

THE LESSON

When you prepare a budget, you plan how to spend your money over the coming months or years. A budget also helps you recognize the opportunity costs of your choices. How you view opportunity costs will directly affect your ability to create a budget and more importantly, live with it. Successful budgeting yields freedom from debt, control over finances and attainment of long-term goals. Recognize that there is no free lunch. That lunch may taste good now, but if you overspend, you will pay for it, one way or another. Your gains from budgeting are ultimately more valuable than your opportunity costs.

> *I DIDN'T CARE HOW MUCH WORK IT WOULD TAKE, AND I DIDN'T SEE THE TIME INVESTED AS A WASTE OR LIKE I WAS MISSING OUT ON ANYTHING.*
> *— Misty Copeland*

How many hours do you think Misty Copeland devoted to classes and exercises to develop the body and grace of a prima ballerina? How many times during her formative years do you think she turned down party invitations because she had to rehearse? How many times did she choose meals for their purely nutritional sake compared to, say, a mouthwatering double-patty cheeseburger with fries?

We don't know the answers to these questions. Perhaps Misty doesn't ether. More often than not though, she decided that whatever price she paid to reach her goal was a price she was willing to pay.

She paid the price of innumerable opportunity costs over many years, but she gained worldwide recognition, adulation, and the priceless sense of accomplishment.

For Misty Copeland and everyone else who archives goals, budgets are simply tradeoffs: opportunity costs vs desired goals.

She budgeted her time, energy, money and calories. Those budgets, like all budgets, are a comparison between what you could do with what you must do.

Creating a budget simply means you are aware of the tradeoff. Living with the budget means you have finally accepted that what you gain with a budget is more valued than what you lose in other opportunities.

If the pain you feel for forsaking opportunities is greater than the reward for forsaking them, your budget will simply be an unfulfilled wish.

If you want to see the heart and soul of successfully managing opportunity costs, just watch Misty Copeland dance.

SUNK COSTS

A sunk cost is an economic concept describing something you have already paid and cannot recover. Such costs exert pressure on today's decisions, affecting tomorrow's outcome. But decisions *should* be made based on future considerations, not yesterday's costs.

Suppose you bought tickets to a football game. This is a sunk cost. If it is raining or cold on game day, the fact that you bought tickets may pressure you to attend the game, knowing full well that you will be wet, cold and generally miserable. The money you spent on the ticket distorts a decision you are making today.

Similarly, if you are already at the game, it does not mean you have to stay there just because you bought the tickets, paid for parking and fought traffic just to get there. The ticket and parking expense, plus the time spent on the road, are all sunk costs.

Suppose you spent $1,000 to fix your car. Your mechanic tells you that you need new brakes that will cost another $200. The $1,000 you previously spent should not matter to you; it's a sunk cost. What matters is only the $200 for the new brakes and peace of mind knowing that they'll stop your car when you need them to.

Finally, suppose you spent $5,000 to buy a stock. It is a sunk cost and it should be irrelevant to any future decision to sell (ignoring the impact on your taxes, anyway). What matters are the stock's price today and its future prospects; only these should affect your selling decision, not what you paid for it.

THE LESSON

Don't fall for the "sunk cost fallacy" that says you have to continue doing something because of the money you have already spent doing it. Today's decision should only consider a) today's additional expense and b) the benefits you will gain from today's expense. If the benefits exceed today's expense, do it and ignore the sunk costs. Don't be afraid to admit you made a *past* mistake. As an investor, don't be afraid to take a loss; don't allow a 40-percent loss to become an 80-percent loss.

> *THERE ARE ONLY TWO LASTING BEQUESTS WE CAN HOPE TO GIVE CHILDREN. ONE OF THESE IS ROOTS, THE OTHER WINGS.*
> — Johann Wolfgang von Goethe

Roots and wings, what a powerful metaphor.

Roots ground us, give us stability, provide a sense of permanence and a link to a past. Wings give us the ability to soar, to move beyond where we are today and to achieve our fullest potential.

The most emotionally secure and mature people you know are those who were raised by families where roots were cherished and nurtured, creating a foundation for growth and development.

For some people, however, roots were more than stabilizing, nurturing and grounding; they were chains. Rather than positive and enabling, they were suppressing and immobilizing. When that happened, wings were never allowed to soar. Low self-esteem, fear of failure, and living in the past are examples of suppressing and immobilizing roots.

We all have histories. Those histories represent the roots of our current beliefs, behaviors and aspirations. We cannot change those roots. They are what they are. They are the sunk costs of our upbringing – the totality of the good times and bad, of our sorrows and joys.

But just as the fallacy of sunk costs teaches us to make current financial decisions independent of past expenditures, so too does it reinforce the power of Goethe's charge to soar into the future.

We created this book on the foundation of yin-and-yang philosophy, a fusion of complementary forces. Roots and wings are a compelling example of that fusion. We all have a past, and, if we are fortunate, we all have a future. But we will only realize a desired future if we appreciate our positive roots and break away from our negative roots.

Soar into the future!

CHAPTER 2

FINANCIAL LITERACY FOR INVESTING

You have money and you want to invest it, so what issues and options should you consider as you make those investments? At the heart and soul of financial literacy, perhaps the most basic lesson is that all investments are risky. The following yins and yangs will help you identify, recognize, and manage those risks as you devise a strategy that blends financial and personal enrichment - a portfolio of *total wealth*.

BONDS

There are two major categories of <u>assets</u> for investors: <u>stocks</u> and bonds. Bonds are issued by borrowers such as corporations, governments, or municipalities. When you buy a newly issued bond, you are acting as an investor, lending money to the issuer.

When you own a bond, you will receive two types of <u>cash flows</u>: interest and principal. Every six months (usually), bonds pay interest. These semiannual payments are also called "coupons" or "coupon interest." Interest is computed by multiplying the coupon interest rate by the bond principal.

The other cash flow is the bond principal (also called par value, maturity value or face value), usually $1,000 for bonds bought by individual investors. The bond principal is paid to you on the day that the loan is repaid. That day is called the maturity date of the bond.

You pay an initial price for the bond, which you might buy from an "issuer," (the first-time seller), or from another investor in what is called the "secondary market." In other words, bonds have <u>liquidity</u>; they can be bought and sold.

As a bond investor, you are exposed to two major <u>risks</u>: interest rate risk (if interest rates rise, bond prices fall) and default risk (if the issuer is unable to repay the interest and/or principal). U.S. Treasury bills, notes and bonds have no default risk; municipal and corporate bonds do. Credit rating agencies, such as Moody's and Standard & Poor's, rate bonds based on their default risk. In general, bonds are considered less risky than stocks. Because they are less risky, investors should expect to earn a lower <u>rate of return</u> on bonds than on stocks.

THE LESSON

Because of <u>diversification</u>, bonds should be part of most investment portfolios, While they are less risky than stocks, bond values will fall if interest rates rise. Long-term bonds are particularly vulnerable to interest rate risk; they can drop precipitously in value if interest rates rise. We believe it's safe to buy individual U.S. Treasury securities. But corporate and municipal bonds have many complex features and are exposed to default risk. Therefore, do not buy individual corporate and municipal bonds; instead, indirectly invest in these types of bonds through <u>mutual funds and ETFs</u>.

> *I DON'T LIKE MONEY ACTUALLY,*
> *BUT IT QUIETS MY NERVES.*
> *— Joe Louis*

Financial security means different things to different people, and it can indeed "quiet the nerves." For some, it means having six months of income in the bank to cover emergency expenses. For others, it means a guaranteed income every month for as long as they live. For still others, it means investments with minimal risk.

Investing in bonds is likely to be a default strategy for those with a low tolerance for risk, and who like the predictability of receiving coupon interest every six months.

Yet, we also define financial security emotionally as well as monetarily. Some people want to "experience" their wealth, enjoying it through all five of their senses. You might not buy a pair of $1,000 shoes, a scarf for $800 or a $1,700 bottle of wine, even if you could afford it. But others can, would, and do.

What we do with our wealth, to feel financially and emotionally secure, are ultimately personal choices, driven by spending and investment options and psychological needs.

Chances are you might get a little defensive when people tell you how to spend your money, unless they are your financial advisors. Extend this logic. Telling other people how to spend *their* money when they have the finances to make decisions without debt (or guilt) is likely to make them defensive.

Because of moral, religious, and cultural influences, we have no trouble telling people how to spend their money. But before you do, walk a mile in the other person's shoes, whether those shoes are torn sneakers or $2,000 Italian imports. How they spend their money is quieting their nerves.

Bottom line: If their spending inflicts pain on others, your judgment may be appropriate. But if it doesn't, let them enjoy their financial security. And we hope you enjoy yours.

STOCKS

The two major <u>asset</u> classes for investors, and financing vehicles for corporations, are stocks and <u>bonds</u>.

Common stock investors are part owners in a corporation. If you buy one share of Apple, you own about 0.00000000006 of Apple. (There are about 17.5 billion shares of Apple outstanding.) Common stock is also called equity. Preferred stock is another type of stock. It is a hybrid security, combining both stock and bond features. Most companies do not issue preferred stock.

As a stockholder, you are entitled to <u>dividends</u> (but not all companies pay dividends), and you may get to vote on decisions – who will serve on the board of directors, merger and acquisition approval, and issuing additional shares of stock. As an owner, you will periodically get a proxy statement asking you to vote on these and other issues.

In the event of a <u>bankruptcy</u>, stockholders are supposed to be last in line to get whatever is distributed by the courts during liquidation. Usually, stockholders get nothing.

Investors buy stock to receive dividends and to realize <u>capital gains</u> (price appreciation). Stocks are risky; because investors dislike <u>risk</u>, stocks are priced to provide a "risk premium," a return over and above the <u>yield</u> offered by treasury securities. Over 93 years ending in 2019, the U.S. historical risk premium has been 8.55 percent per year. In other words, investors in U.S. stocks earned on average 8.55 percent over the Treasury bill rate. But the past does not guarantee the future.

THE LESSON

If you are thinking of buying individual common stocks (we prefer <u>mutual funds</u> and ETFs with low expense ratios), investigate before you invest. Don't fall for tips from unknown individuals who recommend unknown penny stocks. Buy and hold for the long run and invest in quality corporations. Don't invest just because stocks are rising; don't succumb to FOMO (fear of missing out) rallies. <u>Diversify</u>. Rebalance your portfolio when appropriate. Have a strong stomach, because stocks sometimes plummet in value. Between 2000 and 2002 (bursting of the dot.com bubble), U.S. stocks fell 46 percent. In 2008, they declined 38 percent. But U.S. stocks have always come back to reward investors in the long run. We think stock investing will be a worthwhile bet in the future, and for the future.

> *KNOW WHAT YOU OWN AND*
> *KNOW WHY YOU OWN IT.*
> — *Peter Lynch*

Peter Lynch managed the Magellan Mutual Fund between 1977 and 1990, producing a 29.2 percent average annual rate of return. To compare that performance in the sports world, think Ted Williams in baseball, Jack Nicklaus in golf and Michael Jordan in basketball.

Although Lynch is referring specifically to stock ownership, his wisdom applies to ownership in general, and the implication of what it means to own something.

Much of what we own is tangible – a car, a house, furniture, clothes, and a host of other "stuff." Those tangibles have varying degrees of financial and intrinsic value, requiring varying degrees of our attention and concern.

But you also own an invaluable intangible that has profound impact on your journey through life – your behavior. To live a life of purpose, heart and soul means that you realize you are not what you believe, but what you *do*. You own your behavior.

When you own your behavior...

You accept that you have free will and are the agent of your own fate.
You understand that you are the only person on this earth you can control.
You accept responsibility for what you have done. You apologize and seek forgiveness when you should.
You admit your infallibility and learn from your mistakes.

Finally, consider the second part of the Lynch quote, the why. You own your behavior because it enhances self-esteem and engenders respect from others. You will be proud, and others will be proud to know and love you.

When you own your behavior, you are on your way to achieving *total wealth*.

ASSET ALLOCATION

Asset allocation, at its most basic level, is deciding how to spread (allocate) the risk across your investment portfolio: stocks vs. less-risky instruments such as bonds and certificates of deposit (CDs). These decisions will be the primary determinant of your investment performance; i.e., your portfolio's rate of return.

Beyond this seemingly simple decision, you must consider how much to invest in domestic stocks, international stocks and emerging markets stocks, how much in value stocks and growth stocks, how much in large cap stocks and small cap stocks.

You must also decide whether some industries and sectors should be emphasized and if any should be shunned.

Within the asset class of debt instruments, you must decide how much to allocate to long-term and short-term securities, riskless treasuries, slightly risky investment grade corporates and riskier high-yield debt, taxable bonds and municipal bonds, domestic and foreign bonds. Finally, you must decide how much cash to hold.

THE LESSON

You are unique. Your asset allocation decisions reflect your uniqueness: age, level of risk aversion, tax status, health, whether you have dependents, and other personal factors. In addition, your decisions should change as you age. Stocks are risky. Therefore younger investors should invest more in stocks; a typical basic asset allocation for a 30-year-old might be as high as 95 percent in stocks. A 70-year-old with a modest amount of wealth might only be 30-50 percent in stocks. If the stock market were to decline by 60 percent, a younger person can work longer and save over many years to recoup market losses; an older person close to retirement has fewer options. As you spread your money over different types of assets, you will also achieve the benefits of diversification. An investment advisor can guide you through these decisions. Choose the advisor and the allocation wisely.

The wisdom of Marie Kondo's quote speaks to simplifying our life: what do we own and why do we own it? She has become an international star for spreading the intuitively simple message that tidying up improves our life.

In the absence of tidying up we feel both physically emotionally burdened, we literally and figuratively live in clutter. According to Kondo, we have more stuff, but less joy. Deciding what to keep and what to remove should be based on a simple question: Regardless of how I felt about this object in the past, does it bring me joy today?

Financial advisors are not likely to equate asset allocation with tidying up, but that is exactly what you are doing when deciding when and how to rearrange your portfolio. You are essentially simplifying your portfolio to create the greatest value.

Deciding what to buy, what to sell, what weight to give to certain assets vs. other assets, will reduce your emotional stress while providing clarity and focus. You will feel less burdened.

Here's a common question financial advisors ask their clients: Given your current asset allocation are you able to sleep peacefully at night? If not, that portfolio is burdening you. True, your portfolio may gain or lose in value on any given day, but if you have tidied up your assets, the long-term effect will be more joyful than painful.

Simplify your life...you'll sleep better.

DIVERSIFICATION

With diversification, you build a portfolio of several different types of <u>assets</u>, reducing your <u>risk</u> of losing your total investment on any one of them.

In any given year, the values of different assets don't move together. Maybe <u>stocks</u> rise while <u>bonds</u> fall. Maybe real estate rises while stocks fall. Maybe Apple common stock rises in value while the price of Merck common stock falls. This lack of correlation (things zig when other things zag) creates diversification benefits.

Standard deviation is a statistical measure of dispersion. If you randomly chose one stock, the average standard deviation of your return is about 40 percent. If you combine the 500 stocks in the S&P 500 into one portfolio, the standard deviation might be about 18 percent. Thus because of diversification, the portfolio cuts the dispersion of outcomes by half. As the volatility in your portfolio declines, so will your risk.

Consider this hypothetical example: Only one of two companies will develop a vaccine for a given virus. The one that does will double in price while the loser will lose 50 percent of its value. You don't know which company will succeed; it's 50-50. Do you buy one of the stocks? You may pick the wrong stock. Why not diversify and invest in both? If you do, you will make 25 percent no matter the outcome.

THE LESSON

Roulette players place multiple bets on the spin of the wheel. Similarly, bettors at the horse races often place multiple bets on the same race. They are applying the same logic that investors follow when diversifying their portfolio. Spreading the risk across your bets reduces the risk of losing on a single bet. Yes, it is true: putting all your eggs in one basket is indeed risky. ♪

One of the defining qualities of life, a quality that is exciting and adventurous for some while frightening and inhibiting for others, is that life is uncertain, unpredictable and at times chaotic. Because it is unpredictable, we look for ways to buffer the shocks of potential losses – large and small, monetary, and non-monetary.

Yes, variance is inevitable, but failure because of that variance is not. We can create buffers. These buffers define our comfort zone. Insurance, security systems, prenuptial agreements and yes portfolio diversification, are examples of buffering uncertainty and shocks.

Success both "mild" and "wild" is possible. Mild success is manageable and attainable and the goal of many. "Skills and labor" will go a long way in finding and executing those buffers, resulting in "mild success."

Staying within your comfort zone makes sense when you invest your money or are confronting a life-or-death scenario. However, getting out of that comfort zone makes sense if you want to achieve your full potential.

Yet "wild success" is the goal of those willing to take the risk - seizing and capitalizing on the unpredictable and the chaotic. Wild success can far exceed our dreams and fulfill our most fervent hopes.

Experiencing what life has to offer is found on the other side of your comfort zone...the zone of "wild success." Mild versus wild success; you decide on the risk and live with the consequences of that decision.

RISK AND RISK AVERSION

Risk may be defined in both financial terms and psychological terms.

The major financial definition of risk is volatility. A stock that frequently rises and falls by 5 percent per day is riskier than a stock that rises and falls by 1 percent per day. Standard deviation and variance are measures of volatility; the higher they are, the wider is the dispersion or range of outcomes. The higher the volatility, the greater the risk.

Beta, another definition of financial risk, measures volatility by assessing a stock's fluctuations relative to the market. If a stock tends to rise and fall by 15 percent when the market rises and falls by 10 percent, its beta is 1.5. The stock is 50 percent more volatile than the market. Beta incorporates not only standard deviation, but also correlation, which measures how assets' returns move together. The benefit of portfolio diversification results from low correlation.

An estimate of future volatility is the Chicago Board Options Exchange's Volatility Index (VIX). This index is computed from option prices and is also called "the fear index." The VIX was 80 in October 2008, when the country was at the bottom of the great recession caused in part by the mortgage crisis. In March 2020, the start of the COVID pandemic, it was 66. In 2017, when the economy was growing and unemployment was low, the VIX dipped below 10.

Psychologically, financial risk refers to your emotional comfort/discomfort with the possibility of losing money. You are "risk averse" if the pain of an investment loss is greater than the joy of an investment gain. The more risk averse you are, the less you should allocate to risky assets like stocks.

THE LESSON

Your attitude toward risk may be *the* major determinant of your asset allocation decision. Your financial advisor probably gave you a short questionnaire to measure your risk aversion. If you don't have an advisor, or have not completed such a questionnaire, google "risk aversion questionnaire" and see what some of these online surveys say about your level of risk aversion. Don't bear more risk than you can handle. If you are losing sleep, you are exposed to too much risk. Always expect to be compensated for bearing risk. But recognize that your expectations won't always be met.

> *IN MY OWN LIFE, AS THE NEARER I GET*
> *TO THE END OF LIFE ON THIS EARTH,*
> *THE SIMPLER I WANT TO BECOME.*
> — *Fred Rogers*

These are the bottom-line questions if you are managing your own finances: Why are you managing your finances? What is your goal?

If your goal is to build a portfolio, defined as a financial target, by a target date, you are likely to focus on numbers, calendars, apps, indices and data-driven market projections. Your planning focuses on data, and your outcome will be defined by data – albeit financial data. Your target will be a financial number.

But others answering the bottom-line question define their goal not as a number but as an event, an experience, a dream, even a celebration. For those people, the goal is not money *per se*, but how that money will be used.

For example, they might say that they need to create college funds for the kids, to buy a retirement home in the mountains, to live care-free while sailing on a private boat or to create a financial legacy for a favorite charity.

Obviously, these goals require money, but money is not the driving force. The dreams and aspirations are the drivers. Creating the financial portfolio is the means, not the ends.

Defining financial goals in terms of means vs. ends adds an intriguing perspective on risk and risk aversion. If you are a speculator you may have a higher risk tolerance because all you are losing is money. But if you are an investor building a portfolio for future celebration and life-cycle events, you are losing more than money; you are losing dreams.

Understand the difference between a portfolio as ends versus means, and a portfolio as means versus ends. Once you understand the difference, you will know why many are financially rich but spiritually bankrupt.

DERIVATIVES

A derivative is a financial contract whose value is "derived from," or depends on, the price of an <u>asset</u>, called the "underlying asset." There are four basic types of derivative contracts: forwards, futures, swaps and <u>options</u>.

For example, the value of an option on 100 shares of Microsoft <u>stock</u> depends on the price of Microsoft. The value of a futures contract (see <u>commodities</u>) on 1,000 barrels of oil depends on changes in the price of oil. The value of a forward contract on a million euros (the European currency) depends on changes in the price of a euro. The value of an "interest rate swap" depends on whether interest rates rise or fall.

Derivatives are indispensable tools for large corporations, <u>mutual funds</u>, farmers and others to manage their <u>risk.</u> As such, they are used to <u>hedge</u> (protect) against unwanted price risk. They also are used by many investors to speculate (bet on) price increases or decreases of the underlying asset.

The size of the many derivatives markets around the world is difficult to measure, but it is beyond huge. By one common measure, it approaches one quadrillion dollars!

THE LESSON

Trading in derivatives impacts the prices of stocks, interest rates, foreign currencies, and <u>commodities</u>. They also affect all individual investors, businesses, and governments. However, derivatives are sophisticated instruments, and almost all the large and experienced traders know much more about them than you do. Unless you invest a lot of time learning about them (and have a high tolerance for risk), we don't recommend you trade them. If your <u>financial advisor</u> recommends that you use them for speculation, we strongly urge you to consider "swapping" advisors. ♪

Someone once said that common sense is indeed uncommon. But what is common sense? More importantly, why is it so uncommon?

Common sense means that you know there are inherent risks in simply living day to day, and you live your life taking chances. But you take those chances with street smarts; you assess situations prudently and act accordingly.

Common sense means that you know what you know, and you know what you don't know. You don't try to fake understanding just so you'll look smart.

Common sense means that you learn from your mistakes. We all make mistakes; that's the risk we take by simply living. But not all of us repeat the same mistake over and over. Those who do lack common sense.

In short, common sense means that you know you are a work in progress.

There's a reason why common sense is uncommon: We are creatures of habit more than creatures of change. Many of us fail to learn from our mistakes; we fail to acknowledge our weaknesses or accurately assess situations.

Which brings us to the heart and soul of trading in derivatives.

Obviously assessing complex trades requires intelligence and quantitative skills, but it also requires common sense. That means an acceptance of what you know and don't know. Derivatives test more than your book smarts; they also test your street smarts – the essence of common sense.

Loretta Lynn, one smart lady. That coal miner's daughter could have bought a dozen coal mines!

OPTIONS: CALLS AND PUTS

Options are sophisticated <u>derivative</u> contracts. There are two types of financial options: puts and calls. A call option gives you the right to buy something in the future at a specified price. A put option gives you the right to sell something in the future at a specified price. Options give you flexibility to act, but only if it is in your best interest to act. You are not obligated to buy or sell.

Options are rights, not obligations, and that has value. Aside from flexibility, options also provide <u>leverage</u> because you get exposure to the <u>asset</u> at a fraction of the cost of buying it. You may pay $11,500 to buy 100 shares of Apple <u>stock</u>, but a call option giving you the right to buy 100 shares of Apple anytime in the next three months, for $115/share, might cost you only $950.

If Apple's stock price rises by 20 percent in the next three months, you might make 140 percent on your call option; if Apple declines in value, just don't exercise your right to buy. Your maximum loss on the call option (if Apple's price remains unchanged or declines) is limited to $950. While unlikely (because Apple's stock price would have to drop to zero), your maximum potential loss on the stock is $11,500.

You might be fortunate and work for a company that compensates key employees with stock options. These are call options given to you as a form of compensation; they typically give you the option to buy your company's stock in the future at a specified price…. usually equal to its current price. If the stock price rises in the next 10 years, the options will have value.

Buying a put option on a stock you own provides <u>insurance</u> against a stock price decline. Like all insurance policies, a put has a cost.

THE LESSON

Research shows that most traders who use options to speculate end up losing money! Small traders compete against more experienced traders who have the advantages of information and trading speed. To make money, you must overcome commissions and the bid-ask spread. It isn't easy. Just remember that playing in the options market proves the old poker saying. "If you don't know who the sucker is, then it's you."

How valuable is someone capable of recognizing and executing winning options? Almost half a billion dollars.

In July 2020, the Kansas City Chiefs signed Patrick Mahomes, the 2018 NFL MVP, to a 10-year, $450-million contract extension worth up to $500 million with incentives. Not bad.

Obviously, professional athletes compete for salary and fringe benefits in a very different economic market than the average Mary, Mark or Jose. Yet the principle of linking compensation to exceptional skill and talent holds true regardless of the market.

In the NFL, quarterbacks who read defenses and can exercise their right (an option) to change a play at the line of scrimmage are valuable; they have a rare skill: they find ways to "make big plays happen." They also "look for the playmakers."

Finding ways to get them in the play is a powerful perspective for understanding how options improve our lives.

You can go through life believing you do not need anyone else, or you have the option to reach out to others. Reaching out is a much better option.

You can go through life believing you have all the answers and what you don't know isn't worth knowing. Or you have the option to accept that there is much you don't know and need to seek wisdom wherever you can find it. Seeking wisdom is a much better option.

You can go through life believing that once you become a millionaire or multi-millionaire you will be happy. Or you have the option of believing that your happiness depends simply on having enough money to fill your needs. Knowing you have enough versus never having enough is a much better option.

Because you have free will you have options. When your options are driven by heart and soul, you will achieve *total wealth*.

COMMODITIES AND FUTURES CONTRACTS

Have you ever called a restaurant to make a reservation for a "prix fixe" (fixed price) dinner? If so, you have entered into a long position in a "forward contract." You have committed to buy something in the future. You have set the price. On a future day, you will pay that price and receive the dinner.

A futures contract, often on a commodity rather than a meal, is like that forward contract. They are commitments to buy or sell something in the future at a price that is determined today. The "something," called the "underlying asset," might be an agricultural commodity like wheat or corn, a metal (gold or silver), an energy product (oil or natural gas), a fixed income instrument (treasury bonds), a foreign currency or a basket of stocks like the 500 that make up the S&P 500 Index.

Commodities trade on futures exchanges such as the Chicago Mercantile Exchange (CME). The futures contracts are standardized, meaning that the asset behind every contract is the same: the same amount (e.g., 100 ounces of gold), the same quality, with precise information about how, where and when delivery will take place.

Futures traders are categorized as "speculators" or "hedgers." Speculators buy (go long) futures contracts when they believe the price of the underlying asset will rise, and sell (go short) when they believe the price will decline.

But the usefulness of futures trading exists because of the parties who use the contracts to hedge their risk exposure. For example, wheat farmers may fear that the price of their crops will decline prior to harvest, so they sell wheat futures to lock in the price on the harvest day. Similarly, airlines may fear that the price of jet fuel will increase in the future, so they buy crude oil futures contracts to lock in the future cost of their fuel.

THE LESSON

Futures contracts are complex and risky. Proceed with caution (if you proceed at all). In particular, you must know when and how to make delivery (sell) or take delivery (buy) of the underlying asset. For this reason, we don't recommend you trade futures. But recognize that for hedgers, futures are an important means for managing risks. Virtually every large corporation, bank, and mutual fund trades futures contracts, usually for a good reason.

> *THE MEEK SHALL INHERIT THE EARTH,*
> *BUT NOT THE MINERAL RIGHTS.*
> — J. Paul Getty

When we think of today's famous entrepreneurs, a predictable set of names comes to mind: Bill Gates and Paul Allen, Steve Jobs and Steve Wozniak, Jeff Bezos, Elon Musk, Larry Page and Sergey Brin, and Mark Zuckerberg. The common link across these names is that they created immense wealth for themselves and early investors by launching companies that built the infrastructure for our high-tech, information-driven world.

If you go back to the late 19th and early 20th centuries you would also see a predictable set of entrepreneurs: Rockefeller, Carnegie, Vanderbilt, Gould, Harriman, and Ford. They too, have a common link: railroads, oil, steel, autos, and shipping. Their companies established the physical infrastructure of America.

What both groups have in common is what characterizes all entrepreneurs: a vision driven, not by creating personal wealth, but by creating something new, something important and something valuable to others. Wealth was the byproduct of their vision, not the goal.

Let's be honest, commodities are soulless. Oil, soybeans, pork bellies or any other product traded in commodity markets equate to dollars and cents, not heart and emotions. But the farmers who plant and harvest crops, who feed and care for livestock, and the visionaries who built the mining companies and drilling operations are the embodiment of the heart and soul of commodities.

Whether you trade in commodity futures is a personal choice. But if you do, realize that you are trading a commodity that represents the blood, sweat, tears and vision of someone who enabled you to make a trade. Those visionaries are anything but "meek."

Finally, remember that commodities are inanimate. People are not; they have hearts and souls. If you treat them as if they are commodities you lose your heart and soul.

HEDGING

A hedge is created when an investor takes opposite positions in two similar investments, the purpose being to reduce the exposure to unwanted changes in prices. Hedge funds first got their name because their earliest traders would buy shares in one company (e.g., Ford) while simultaneously selling short a similar stock on which it was bearish (e.g., GM). The short position was an attempt to hedge the long position.

Futures contracts and other derivatives are often used to create a hedge. For example, a mutual fund or ETF might own a large well diversified portfolio of stocks. To hedge against a feared stock market decline, the mutual fund might sell futures contracts on the S&P500 Index. If the stock market does decline, the value of the stocks owned by the fund will decline, but it will earn a profit on the short futures position.

As another example, a multinational corporation may need to buy millions of euros, the currency that is used in most of Europe, to conduct its business operations in the coming year. Because it worries that the price of a euro will increase, it hedges by buying futures contracts on euros today. If the price of euros does go up, the firm will pay more for its euros during the next year, but during that time it will also earn a profit on the long futures position.

In each case, if the hedge performed well, the firm eliminates most of the price risk it faced from its unhedged position.

THE LESSON

Hedging reduces risk, but it's a double-edged sword. Yes, there is a chance that a price increase will cause you distress (like with the euro example above), so you will want to lock in your purchase price today. But you could be wrong; prices might go down. If you hedged, you will not benefit from that price decrease. In other words, the mutual fund that hedged will be pleased that it hedged if stock prices do decline, but it will be unhappy it hedged if prices end up rising. Your goal of hedging is to reduce risk, not to make money. If you want to hedge, we recommend hiring an expert to provide guidance. Insurance is a form of hedging, but it can be costly.

> *IF YOU BREAK YOUR NECK, IF YOU HAVE NOTHING TO EAT, IF YOUR HOUSE IS ON FIRE, THEN YOU GOT A PROBLEM. EVERYTHING ELSE IS INCONVENIENCE.*
> — Robert Fulghum

This is an indisputable fact in creating *Your Total Wealth*: you will be constantly assessing risks and considering options for controlling it or compensating for a potential loss.

Whether assessing the risks of an investment or the risks of managing your personal life, you are asking a fundamental question: What can I do to make sure I don't lose what is important to me? Or if I must lose, what can I do to make sure I don't lose too much?

What we do to control a potential loss is an example of hedging. That is why we are cautious when driving a car, buying health insurance, checking food ingredients (especially if we have allergies) or buying a smoke detector for the house.

Prudence, emotional maturity and foresight wouldn't have it any other way.

But Fulghum's perspective on "problem" versus "inconvenience" raises an intriguing issue. He is telling us that we might find ourselves investing too much time, money and energy in covering a loss that really isn't a problem – just an inconvenience.

For example, the 2020 coronavirus pandemic saw some consumers load up on toilet paper and spaghetti to hedge their bets about a shortage, while others saw that behavior as irrational hoarding. The former saw an emergency for which they prepared. The latter thought they were making the problem worse by acting irrationally.

Problem or inconvenience? Rational response or irrational response? Hedging a risk or simply overreacting?

Both the Fulghum quote, and the question it poses, cut to the core of assessing risk and planning for potential loss. If you are confronted with a problem that could create a loss, consider options for covering that loss.

But if you are dealing with an inconvenience, buckle up, smile, and say, "This too shall pass."

ALTERNATIVE FINANCIAL INVESTMENTS

Typical investments include stocks and bonds. Alternative financial investments are atypical, such as real estate, private equity and hedge funds.

Many individuals invest in real estate beyond their personal residence. They buy rental property (residential or commercial) or land. Others take a more passive approach, through real estate investment trusts (REITS), which are like mutual funds; they pool the money of many investors to buy real estate. REITS offer liquidity, since you can buy and sell shares when you want. Physical real estate lacks liquidity.

There are two forms of private equity: venture capital and buyout funds. Venture capital is pooled money invested in startups. Many publicly traded corporations, including Facebook, Groupon and Google, got their start from venture capitalists.

Buyout funds pool investor money to buy shares of well-established companies. Once these buyout funds own most of the shares, the targeted firms are said to have been "taken private." Their shares no longer trade on stock exchanges. Often, large corporations are taken private using enormous borrowing, hence the term "leveraged buyout," known by its acronym, LBO.

Hedge funds are unregulated pools of money from wealthy "accredited investors" who meet requirements based on income, wealth or professional experience and knowledge. The original hedge funds were "long-short" funds; they bought shares (went long) in companies expected to perform well, and at the same time, sold short shares in other companies expected to underperform.

For example, a long-short hedge fund might buy shares in Tesla (green technology of the future), and at the same time sell short shares of Ford (fossil-fuel burning internal combustion engines). But since they are unregulated, hedge funds can invest in anything they want.

THE LESSON

Alternative investments demand considerable wealth and knowledge. To invest in private equity funds and hedge funds you must be an accredited investor with investment savvy. Alternatives tend to be risky; some have performed well while others have tanked, wiping out investors. If you follow sound diversification principles, limit your portfolio to 5-10 percent in alternative investments at most, and only if you have a substantial amount invested in typical investments. We focused on financial alternatives, but if you invest in valuable collectibles that you enjoy (art, antiques, comic books), keep investing!

We are all creatures of habit. In fact, the only reason mass marketing works is because marketers pool data across demographic groups, analyze it with sophisticated tools, and based on that analysis, predict what you are likely to buy, why you buy it, how much you are likely to spend. They know your habits.

Our habitual patterns also explain investment behavior: why we invest, how much we invest, and our investment choices. Yet every now and then we see or are offered an investment opportunity that challenges our routine.

You better believe many people right now are still agonizing because they had an opportunity to be an early investor in Facebook, Microsoft, Google, or Apple, *and turned it down.*

But there were also many who jumped at the chance. They didn't ask where they would sit after being offered a seat on the rocket ship, they just got on.

At the end of your life, you'll probably ponder any regrets you might have. Based on considerable psychological research, you'll regret not being courageous when you should have been. High up on the list of heart-wrenching regrets is not saying what should have been said, and not doing what should have been done. Life presents us with options, and continually tests our courage.

Live courageously and with the knowledge that regardless of the outcome you can and will survive.

CRYPTOCURRENCY

Cryptocurrency is a digital asset that can serve as a medium of exchange; i.e., a currency. Cryptocurrency is created by a few individuals who verify transactions made by others. Traditional currencies such as the U.S. dollar or the euro are created by central banks – in the United States, the Federal Reserve Bank.

Bitcoin was the first cryptocurrency. Launched in 2009, it was reputedly created by someone named Satoshi Nakamoto, of whom little is known. By 2019 well over 2,000 cryptocurrencies had been created, most of which were trading on exchanges like any conventional currency. Bitcoin is created when an equation, or puzzle, is solved; the process of solving the equations is called "mining."

Mining requires enormous computational power and electricity. In 2019, bitcoin energy usage was estimated to use 0.28 percent of the world's supply of electricity. When a miner solves a sufficient number of the puzzles, she receives a small fraction of a bitcoin.

Bitcoin is based on blockchain, a decentralized and transparent ledger (the database of transactions) shared by participants in a cryptocurrency, allowing the verification of all transactions in that cryptocurrency. This makes it difficult (perhaps impossible) for fraud or counterfeiting to occur. The blockchain is, in a sense, a linked chain of transactions data. The puzzles that miners solve are transaction confirmations.

There are no physical cryptocurrencies; they are all online. If you lose the key (a password) to your digital wallet, you may lose your cryptocurrency.

THE LESSON

Cryptocurrencies are extremely controversial. For every ardent fan of cryptocurrencies, there is a doomsayer convinced that they will ultimately prove to be nearly worthless. Frankly, we don't know what they are. Maybe bitcoin and the interest in cryptocurrencies will grow. Maybe there is value to cryptocurrencies. Maybe they are the 21st century equivalent to gold. The value of bitcoin peaked at over $18,000 in late 2017. But its price is very volatile. A year later, its value was $3,200. At the beginning of 2021, bitcoin was trading at over $40,000! Because cryptocurrencies are not created by a centralized government, we believe the risk in owning them is not worth taking. And be wary of scammers who pitch cryptocurrency opportunities to you. ♪

Cryptocurrency exists, but it doesn't exist. Unlike gold, silver or paper money issued by a central bank, cryptocurrency doesn't have a physical form. It is virtual currency.

Consider for a moment how pervasive virtual reality is. You can buy a house without having stepped inside of it, some houses have been purchased exclusively through virtual tours.

You can attend a meeting without being in the same room with other attendees. During the pandemic of 2020, virtual meetings were the norm, not the exception.

You can have an appointment with your doctor without being in the same room with her. Indeed, virtual health care services may become the default option for non-emergency medical care in the future.

You can do banking in your pajamas, in the comfort of your own home, if you have high-speed connectivity and up-to-date hardware and software.

Finally, you can have human contact without really having human contact. Through social media platforms like Facebook and Twitter, you can have an unlimited number of "friends" and engage in chitchat without ever experiencing the physical presence of those friends.

The heart-and-soul implication of cryptocurrency specifically, and virtual reality generally, is that *technology giveth and technology taketh away.* Clearly, we gain efficiency and cost savings as high-tech solutions solve problems in our new virtual world. But we also lose something.

We lose the emotional bonding people desire in real classrooms, meetings, face-to-face dialogue and doctors' appointments.

Want proof that technology giveth and taketh away? Talk to any bride and groom who were married during the 2020 pandemic, forced by circumstances to exchange vows in real time as family and friends watched on a computer screen. Ask them how they felt about sharing their special day in such a socially distant way.

Ask anyone who said their final goodbyes to a loved one through a smartphone or a laptop.

ANNUITY

An annuity is a series of periodic payments. An ordinary annuity begins one period from "now," each payment is the same amount, with an ending date for the payments. An "annuity due" begins today, rather than one period from today. With a "perpetuity," there is no last payment; they are supposed to go on forever. With a growing annuity, the payments increase in dollar amount over time at a steady rate.

You will deal with annuities throughout your life. Your monthly <u>mortgage</u> payment, auto leases and auto loan payments are annuities (often with an extra initial down payment) you pay to a lender. The <u>dividends</u> you receive on <u>stocks</u> are often modeled to be annuities. Preferred stocks are another security that some companies issue to raise <u>capital</u>. They promise to pay a fixed dividend forever, a "perpetuity," unless something unexpected happens, like a corporate <u>bankruptcy</u>.

Social security payments represent a growing annuity if there is <u>inflation</u>, and an ordinary annuity if there is none. If you retire with a <u>pension</u>, it will be an annuity. Finally, life insurance companies offer many types of annuities.

THE LESSON

Create your own annuity. Get in the habit of saving every month. Better still, save just a bit more each month than the prior month (a growing annuity). Also, carefully research the insurance companies that sell annuities. Find the rating of the insurance company at ratings agencies such as Moody's, A.M. Best, Fitch, and Standard & Poor's. Realize that insurance salespeople make their living from commissions you are (perhaps unknowingly) paying them, which reduces the annuity you will ultimately receive. Beware <u>the agency problem</u>!

If you ever talk to a Marine, whether on active duty or not, you will hear words like pride, loyalty, passion, duty, and commitment. You may even hear the Marine Corps motto in a shortened form: Semper Fi.

Even if that Marine has misgivings about the specific mission they were on, or the country they were in, you will not hear doubts or misgivings about the Corps or their comrades in arm. You are listening to someone describing an *emotional annuity*, and they are likely to have those feelings for as long as they live.

You can also *witness* an emotional annuity. The next time you see an elderly couple walking down the street with smiles on their faces, holding hands and sharing a loving glance, you are witnessing an emotional annuity payment.

A financial annuity is a predictable and often guaranteed payment stream, either for a fixed period or in perpetuity. An emotional annuity is a predictable and yes, guaranteed human bond of caring, commitment and concern. It describes the most loving families and friends. It says, "I'm here. You can count on me."

When parents describe the unconditional love for their children, they are describing an emotional annuity. During the wedding ceremony, when couples promise to love and honor, in sickness and in health, they are committing to an emotional annuity. When adult children take care of aging parents, those children are making an emotional annuity payment.

Semper fidelis is the essence of an emotional annuity. If you have ever experienced it, you are indeed blessed. If you want to experience it, start making the emotional investment today, because time passes quickly. In the words of Lena Horne, *"It's so nice to get flowers while you can still smell the fragrance."*

DIVIDENDS

Many stocks pay dividends, which are periodic (usually quarterly) cash flows to stockholders. Dividends are declared by firms' boards of directors. Dividends can increase over time, decrease or be eliminated.

Firms pay dividends when they have reasonably high profits and cash flow, and they don't need the money to invest in new businesses, products or plant and equipment. Rapidly growing companies tend not to pay dividends or at least very low ones. Profitable firms with fewer growth prospects tend to pay higher dividends.

As of July 2020, there were 66 "dividend aristocrats" in the S&P 500 Index – 66 companies that have paid increasing dividends every year for at least 25 years.

The "dividend yield" is the annual dividend amount divided by the stock price. Stocks with very high dividend yields tend to be risky because the companies are more likely to cut their dividends. Because of this risk, do not "chase yield"; i.e., don't buy a stock simply because it has a very high dividend yield.

THE LESSON

Are you concerned more with dividend income or stock appreciation? Income-oriented (often older) investors prefer stocks with relatively high-dividend yields, believed to be safe from being reduced or eliminated. Growth oriented investors prefer stocks that hold the promise of high capital gains; indeed, they often prefer stocks that don't pay any dividends. Dividends are taxed, while taxes on capital gains can be deferred for as long as you own the stock. Prior to 1950, most of the high rate of return earned by investors in U.S. stocks came from dividends. Since then, capital gains have outpaced dividends.

> *ONE OF THE OLDEST HUMAN NEEDS IS HAVING SOMEONE TO WONDER WHERE YOU ARE WHEN YOU DON'T COME HOME AT NIGHT.*
> — Margaret Mead

What is your favorite holiday? If you are like most people, you probably answered Christmas or Thanksgiving. If it's Christmas, you might have been thinking of gifts, Christmas songs (religious and secular), the anticipation leading up to Christmas day, or the loving chaos of the day itself.

If it's Thanksgiving, you too might have been thinking of the anticipation, maybe reminiscing about the sight and aromas of a turkey dinner, or the contentment of a day devoted to giving thanks.

What's common to both those holidays are memorable times people share with their families. Some will travel thousands of miles just to spend one or both holidays with those they love. So special and heart-warming are these times of the year that many people open their homes to guests, just so they can share their joy with others.

To these people being rich has nothing to do with expensive meals eaten on a silk tablecloth, under the roof of a house in an exclusive neighborhood. Nor does it involve lavish presents.

Deep down, you know that the real present is the laughter and love of those around you. What you experienced during those "rich" moments was a dividend of a loving family.

Not all investments increase in value, some decrease. Not all of them pay dividends. But if you are looking forward to spending Thanksgiving or Christmas with family, you have made a wise investment, indeed.

Continue making that investment and keep looking forward to the dividend. Even if unforeseen events prevent you from sharing the holidays, you will know you are missed, and they know you are missing them.

Time will pass and you will forget about the neatly wrapped presents, but you will forever remember the presence of your family. What a priceless dividend!

INDEX FUNDS

An index fund is a passively managed <u>mutual fund</u>. They don't try to find undervalued securities or actively trade in and out of <u>stocks</u> (or <u>bonds</u>, for bond index funds). They buy a portfolio of securities that replicates an index, such as the S&P500 Index. Then, they hold that portfolio, trading only when necessary (e.g., because a company was acquired by another company). <u>Diversification</u>, their "buy-and-hold" strategy, and low expenses enhance their performance.

There are both index mutual funds, and index <u>ETFs (Exchange Traded Funds)</u>. The primary difference between them is that ETFs let you buy and sell during the day at intraday prices, while mutual fund transactions only occur at end-of-day prices (4 P.M. Eastern Time).

Index funds offer two major benefits: low expenses and diversification. You may want to invest in bank stocks but aren't sure about which individual bank stocks to buy. Instead, buy a bank industry index sector fund. If you are bullish on small cap Japanese stocks, you can buy shares in a Japanese small cap index fund.

Different index funds track different indexes. The index may be domestic (U.S.) or international (e.g., EAFE, which stands for Europe, Australasia, and Far East, an index of all developed markets other than the U.S. and Canada). There are also stock index funds that track different industries, and different market sectors (e.g., large cap vs. small cap).

At the end of 2019, there were almost 500 U.S.-based index mutual funds managing $4.3 trillion in net <u>assets</u>, representing about 25 percent of total (index plus actively managed) U.S.-based mutual fund assets. In contrast, 96 percent of ETF assets were held in index ETFs.

THE LESSON

When deciding between index mutual funds and ETF's, compare their expense ratios, avoid <u>illiquid</u> ETFs that have wide <u>bid-ask spreads</u>, and examine their past performance relative to their benchmark index. Diversify across different broad markets. If you want to select a market segment that you believe will outperform (like biotech), make a side bet and invest a small part of your portfolio in it. *Be very careful* before investing in commodity funds; they can perform erratically and unexpectedly. Also, avoid "leveraged index funds" that include inverse index funds that go up when stocks decline. Avoid 2X and 3X index funds and ETFs, which are supposed to rise or fall two to three times whatever the market does. ♪

> *INVESTING SHOULD BE MORE LIKE WATCHING PAINT DRY OR WATCHING GRASS GROW. IF YOU WANT EXCITEMENT TAKE $800 AND GO TO LAS VEGAS.*
> *— Paul Samuelson*

A Nobel laureate in economics, Paul Samuelson gives us two options: You can invest, or you can gamble. They both come with risks, but with different types of risks. Gambling is unquestionably risky with predictable highs and lows that are not for the faint of heart. Stocks are priced so that you expect to make money. Gambling is set up so that you should expect to lose money.

Investors vs. gamblers.

According to the Las Vegas Convention and Visitors Authority, there were approximately 3.5 million visitors per month in 2019. During that same 12-month period, approximately 500,000 per month attended conventions.

Did every one of those people gamble? Don't bet on it. Did most of those people gamble? That's a good bet. Were any professional gamblers among them? That's a sure bet. Were there some who played a slot machine and maybe a few hands of blackjack, then called it a night? Another sure bet.

Clearly, there are people who never gamble and see it as too risky, maybe even sinful. There are others who want to experience the "fun" of gambling, trying their luck while setting a limit on how much they could lose. Finally, there are those who will bet the farm on a consistent basis. Gambling to them is an addictive high.

If you are a gambler, index funds will put you to sleep, not because you find them restful, but because they bore you.

If you are an investor, you will find index funds an attractive option; they are not as volatile as your average individual stock.

Investing or gambling? Peace of mind or excitement? Security or adrenaline rush? Your long-term future or short-term entertainment? The choices you make go well beyond financial planning. They say something about how you live your life.

MUTUAL FUND SELECTION

Mutual funds and exchange traded funds (ETFs) are investment companies that invest the money of many investors in individual <u>stocks</u> and debt securities, and sometimes <u>commodities</u> and <u>derivatives</u>. In 2019, there were almost 8,000 mutual funds in the U.S., and over 2,000 ETFs.

So how can you choose which fund or ETF is best? Know their differences:

Long term versus short term: For long-term, buy-and-hold investors, there is usually little difference between <u>index funds and index ETFs</u>.

Load versus no load: Avoid mutual funds with "loads," which are expenses added to your purchase price, and/or subtracted from your selling price. Instead, stick with "no-load" mutual funds.

Stocks versus fixed income: For a mix of both, consider "target date funds" that invest in both <u>asset</u> classes, in proportions that are deemed appropriate for your chosen target date. Your target date is a future date when you anticipate you will need your money, often when you retire. Target date funds make the <u>asset allocation</u> decision for you, but if you are very risk averse, be aware that they have been criticized for taking on more investment risk than they should.

Niche or broad: Stock funds might be classified as: a) domestic, international or emerging markets, b) sector funds that invest only in one industry, c) growth or value, with many gradations, d) large-cap, mid-cap or small-cap, defined by market <u>capitalizations</u>, e) high <u>dividend</u> yields or growing dividends, and f) environmental, social and governance (ESG) funds that target stocks of companies that do not pollute, sell healthy products and services, and/or are judged to be socially responsive.

<u>Bond</u> funds can also be classified in many ways: a) money market funds that invest in safe, short term debt, b) government bond funds, perhaps differing on the bonds' maturity, c) corporate bond funds that differ on their default <u>risk</u> or their maturity, and d) domestic, international or emerging market bond funds.

THE LESSON

You have many options for investing in mutual funds because no two investors are alike. Develop a strategy. Know why you are investing and match your funds to that strategy. Your age, level of risk aversion and unique personal circumstances should drive your selection. Choose funds with low expense ratios. High expenses mean you earn less. Few actively managed funds outperform their index benchmarks over long periods of time because of those expenses. ♪

You make hundreds of decisions every day, most of which are minor and of little long-term consequence: What clothes should I wear today? Should I carry an umbrella? What brand of toothpaste should I buy? How best to arrange my closet? What do I want for lunch?

These decisions don't cause sleepless nights or gut-wrenching turmoil.

But there are other decisions that do cause stress – major decisions with life-altering consequences: Should I marry? Whom should I marry? Where do I want to live? How should I support my family? Should I quit my job? Should I get my knee replaced?

Life-altering decisions are indeed difficult, but they are even more agonizing in the absence of personal values. Values are the Why of life; plans and goals are the What and the How.

What is important in your life? What do you hold dear? What is your moral code? How do you define right and wrong, good and bad? The answers to these questions define your values. You will still have to face life-altering issues, but your values will help you make them. They are the guiding principles for living the life you want to live.

They are your north star, your guiding light.

When you don't have these principles, you will still make tough decisions, but those decisions will seem chaotic, ad hoc, and quixotic. They will lack any unifying theme, pattern, or overarching purpose.

They also will have a debilitating consequence: second guessing and self-doubt. You will question why you made the decision. You may start questioning your intelligence and your self-worth.

The absence of guiding principles also creates problems for friends and family. They will not be able to count on you.

Achieving *total wealth* is a journey that begins with WHY, not What and How.

STOCK INDEXES

A stock index measures the performance, or <u>rate of return</u>, of a portfolio of <u>stocks</u>. Indexes differ according to their composition and the relative weighting of the stocks they track.

The composition of indexes varies. The Dow Jones Industrial Average (DJIA) includes just 30 stocks; the NASDAQ Composite Index has more than 2,500. The S&P 500 has – you guessed it – 500 stocks, but the Wilshire 5000, one of the broadest based indexes, has about 3,500. (Go figure.)

There are three primary ways to weight the stocks in an index. The most common is to value-weight, which means that the amount invested in each stock is proportional to its market <u>capitalization</u>. The S&P 500, NASDAQ and Wilshire indexes are all value weighted. As of November 2020, the top five stocks in the S&P 500 – Apple, Microsoft, Google, Amazon and Facebook – made up 23 percent of the index. But they are only 1 percent (5 out of 500) of the actual number of stocks in the S&P 500.

A second method of weighting is equal-weighting. There is an equally weighted version of the S&P 500 index, the S&P EWI, in which each of the component stocks count for 1/500 (0.2 percent) of the index. When small cap stocks perform better than large cap stocks, the S&P EWI will outperform the S&P 500.

The third method of weighting is to price-weight. The DJIA is a price-weighted index. On Sept. 17, 2020, the price of UnitedHealth Group (UNH) was $304.98, while the price of Cisco (CSCO) was $40.37. Thus, UNH's impact on the DJIA was 7.55 times greater than CSCO's impact (304.98/40.37 = 7.55).

There are other less common methods of weighting indexes. Some funds weight indexes by fundamental measures such as <u>dividends</u> (stocks paying the highest dividends have more impact on such an index than stocks with lower dividends).

THE LESSON

You increase your investment savvy by understanding how composition and weighting affect different indexes. Because each index has different securities, and may weight them differently, they provide different views on market performance. There are days that the S&P500 and NASDAQ rise, while the DJIA declines. This happens because a few large cap stocks such as Apple and Microsoft rise, while other high-priced stocks such as UnitedHealth Group decline. If you invest in indexes, invest the time to understand their differences.

In college, you don't major in algebra, you major in math; you don't major in squirrels, but in zoology; not in 1922, but in history.

An academic major is not a specific course; it's a collection of related courses. The labels we assign academic majors help us understand the common themes cutting across those courses.

Consider other common labels for categorizing and grouping.

Job titles: If you tell someone you work in marketing, they get a general description of what you do. They may not know your specific duties, but they know you help promote and sell a product or service.

Political affiliation: If you tell someone you are a Libertarian, they know your general philosophy of the role of government.

Religion: If you describe yourself as an agnostic, people have a general description of whether you believe in a deity.

Labels describing a group of elements help us make quick judgments about that overall group and the specific elements in that group. Unfortunately, if those quick decisions are about specific people, the decision may be faulty, reflecting the essence of Justice Ginsburg's counsel.

A generalization about a group of people based on demographic or psychographic traits is a stereotype. While it may be true that the majority in that group are likely to engage in a certain behavior or share a certain belief, it is not true that any specific person in that group acts that way or thinks that way.

Just as the performance of a stock index does not tell you about the performance of a specific stock, a demographic or psychographic trait will not tell you what a specific person manifesting that trait will or will not do.

Generalizations are risky. Use them judiciously, and with heart and soul.

QUOTES AND ORDERS

When you buy and sell <u>stocks</u>, <u>bonds</u> and <u>ETFs</u>, you may trade with a middleman known as a market maker. A market maker is an individual or firm that quotes a bid price at which she is willing to buy the security, and a higher asked price at which she is willing to sell. She makes a small profit on the bid-ask spread.

When entering an order to trade a security, you must specify the type of order. The two most common are market order and limit order.

Market orders will usually get you the bid price (if you are selling) or the asked price (if you are buying). We say "usually" because quotes can change, some market makers don't reveal their quotes, or because you want to trade more shares than the number of shares offered at the bid or asked price. You may get a better or worse price than the quote you observed. But your order *will* get filled.

With a limit order, you specify the highest price you are willing to pay or the lowest price at which you are willing to sell. *You are not guaranteed that a limit order will be filled*. For example, a stock may be quoted at $20 (bid) to $20.10 (asked). You might enter a limit order to buy at $20.05. Sometimes your order will be filled at your limit price. Sometimes you will even benefit from "price improvement," trading at a price better than what you specified (e.g., buying the stock at $20.04 in the prior example). Sometimes, your order won't be filled.

THE LESSON

If you are going to trade securities, you must know about quotes and orders. Use market orders only when buying or selling actively traded securities with narrow spreads, or when you *really* want to trade the stock and don't care about the price. The latter situation should be rare. Use limit orders when trading less-liquid stocks with wide spreads, recognizing the <u>risk</u> that your order may not be filled; many traders have tried to save a penny or two per share on their limit order, only to lose the order. If you work with a broker or advisor, he should be able to explain the costs and benefits of each order type for the trades you want to make.

Want proof that we are bargaining animals? In 2020, the online auction platform eBay had 182 million users world-wide. Craigslist averaged 95,000 advertised yard sales each week. The size of the 2019 used car market in the United States was $117 billion.

We are not only bargaining animals; we are *voracious* bargaining animals.

But our bargaining goes beyond trades on eBay, yard sales, car lots or even the stock market. We make trades with friends and family daily, and not solely for tangible goods but for social tradeoffs. These trades are psychological contracts – agreements necessary to build, maintain and nurture relationships.

Unlike formal purchase agreements between buyers and sellers, psychological contracts are often unstated and implicit. Rather than written, the terms of a psychological contract are typically (though not always) assumed, implied, and inferred. They are motivated not by profit but by social bonding.

For example:

If you have been living with a spouse or significant other for a long time, you both know the vulnerabilities of one another. You know the topics and issues that will invariably lead to that person's emotional outbursts, and vice versa. You both have learned not to push the other's "hot button." To keep the relationship peaceful, you both have bargained, not to "go there." In other words, you have learned when to keep your mouths shut.

Violating psychological contracts results in predictable outcomes: anger, distrust and possibly severed relationships.

We are indeed bargaining animals. When the trades are between and among family and friends, and involve how we will treat one another, we are experiencing the heart and soul of bargaining.

BEAR MARKET/BULL MARKET

A "bear market" is a declining market; <u>stock</u> prices and values are falling. In the U.S. stock market, many believe that prices must decline by 20 percent or more before it's labeled a bear market. When stocks decline by only 10 to 20 percent, the decline is typically called a "correction." Investors are "bearish" when they believe stock prices will decline.

A "bull market" is a rising market; stock prices and values are rising. After a decline, if prices recover 20 percent of their losses, the market is said to have entered a bull market. "Bullish" investors believe stock prices will rise. Relatedly, you may be said to be bullish if you are optimistic that a good event will occur. You may be bullish about your favorite sports team winning a championship.

In 2020, the market switched from bullish to bearish because of the coronavirus, and back to bullish in a record short period of time. The S&P 500 <u>Index</u> peaked at 3,386 on Feb. 19. The bear market began on March 12, when the S&P 500 Index closed at 2,481 (down more than 20 percent from its high), and it bottomed at 2,237 on March 23. The next bull market began on April 8, when the S&P 500 Index closed at 2,750, up more than 20 percent from its low.

THE LESSON

Are you a trader or an investor? They have different mentalities. The former buys and sells stocks and thinks short term; the latter buys and sells companies and thinks long term. It is often said that the best time to buy stocks is when there is a precipitous drop, and the herd mentality is doom and gloom. Buying when all the news is relentlessly negative has been a very successful long-run investing strategy. But you need a strong stomach to buy at those times. On average, "bottom fishing" is an unprofitable trading strategy; better for you, if you are a trader, to wait for the turnaround to begin. An adage on Wall Street is, "Don't try to catch a falling knife." This adage applies to traders, not long-term investors.

> *IF YOU DON'T STICK TO YOUR VALUES*
> *WHEN THEY ARE BEING TESTED, THEY ARE*
> *NOT VALUES. THEY ARE HOBBIES.*
> *— Jon Stewart*

There were two related issues in our discussion of bear and bull markets. One was a quantitative analysis of market dynamics. The other was a psychological perspective of traders and investors. Some are bullish, optimistic and see rising prices; others are bearish, more pessimistic, and envision falling prices.

A quantitative perspective sees value monetarily, a psychological perspective defines value spiritually and emotionally. The latter perspective is crucial for understanding the tests we face in life and how we perform on those tests.

Some of these tests are administered in school rooms or by potential employers. Those tests assess our abilities, knowledge and talents. Other tests assess our values, the guiding principles of our behavior: what we hold dear, our moral and ethical codes.

These latter tests determine something more important than our academic performance or our ranking as a potential employee: They determine our personal fulfillment.

Our values are tested every day with a fundamental question: Do your behaviors align with your values? When they align, we are on a path towards personal fulfillment and personal growth. Misalignment also defines a path, a path towards self-doubt, pain, and despair. Misalignment means you fail the test, and your values are simply hobbies.

Finally, our values about finances and investing guide decisions resulting in gains or losses, the same goes for our spiritual and emotional values. However, spiritual and emotional losses are far more devastating than financial losses.

Financial markets are cyclical and changing. Your values and the behavior supporting them should not be. We wish you heart, soul, and wisdom as you face and pass your tests.

SHORT SELLING

Normally, you buy a <u>stock</u> (called "going long") and later sell it, hopefully at a higher price. But what if you think a stock is overvalued and that its price will decline? If so, you can "sell short," which means you first sell a stock that you don't own, then buy it back later, hopefully at a lower price. Short sellers are <u>bearish.</u>

How can you sell something that you don't own? Your broker will borrow shares from someone and lend them to you. That someone else will never know his shares are missing. He will continue to get <u>dividends</u>. If he ever needs his shares back – perhaps he wants to sell them – your broker will (almost always) find someone else to borrow the shares from.

Rarely, there will be a "short squeeze," which means that almost everyone wants their shares in their account. If you have sold short, and there is a short squeeze, your broker will require you to buy the shares from someone, but the purchase will likely be at a very high price. Being squeezed can be a horrific event.

Because stocks generally rise in price, selling short is usually a losing bet. Successful short sellers are sophisticated investors who smell fraud or are convinced a stock is in a bubble – wildly overpriced. But the most overpriced stocks (and, indeed, the broad stock market itself) can become even more overpriced and stay overpriced for years. Spotting a bubble may be easier than identifying when the bubble will burst. You may be right in the long run, but a naïve short seller may experience huge losses in the short and intermediate run.

THE LESSON

Don't short sell. It is expensive and you will have to post <u>margin</u>, which means you will get a margin call if you bet wrong. Short sellers are exposed to unlimited losses if the stock rises. If the company pays dividends, you will have to pay them to the individual who loaned you the shares. If you are convinced the market is overpriced, sell some of your stocks. If the market has soared, chances are that your <u>asset allocation</u> to stocks will be excessive; be happy you made money on your stocks and rebalance your portfolio. If you are convinced a stock you own is overpriced, just sell it.

Short sellers are like most traders; they try to buy low and sell high. The only difference is they do it in reverse order; they sell before they buy.

So, do you believe short sellers are pessimistic or optimistic? This is not a trick question; but a question that will get you to rethink your personal definition of pessimism and optimism. You may even rethink which of those two perspectives best describes you.

Our answer is short sellers are both pessimistic *and* optimistic. They believe pessimistically that a stock will drop in price but are optimistic in their belief they will profit from that drop. Moreover, over confidence as either a pessimist or optimist is a common and destructive behavioral bias among investors.

Hmmm …. pessimism and optimism dynamically related and changing as the situation changes. Being pessimistic about some things sometimes, and optimistic about other things at other times. Having one view, pessimistic or optimistic, of the world today may be different than your view of the world tomorrow.

You may say, "but I'm neither an optimist nor a pessimist, I'm a realist." If so, you are implicitly living your life with a yin-and-yang fusion of pessimism and optimism. Indeed, being realistic is neither pessimistic nor optimistic. It is living with and acknowledging pressures, demands and stress, but believing your tomorrows will be better.

All your insurance policies, life, health, auto, home, are example of realism: a fusion of pessimism and optimism.

Caring for and worrying about your dependents, regardless of their ages, is an example of realism: the fusion of pessimism and optimism.

Going to bed tonight worried about tomorrow and waking up tomorrow to live that day is realism.

Your Total Wealth is a yin-and-yang fusion of balancing finances and personal fulfillment in an ever-changing world of good news and bad news.

DOLLAR COST AVERAGING

Suppose you suddenly received $1 million and wanted to invest it all in <u>stocks</u>. (Note that investing everything in stocks may not be your best option; review the concept of <u>asset allocation</u>.) You could invest all of it immediately, and since stocks have risen in two-thirds of the years since 1927, you may even be justified in choosing that route.

But how would you feel if you had invested that money early in 1929 and watched your $1 million shrink to $280,000 in four years? Or if you invested it early in 1973 or early in 2000, only to see your $1 million shrivel to $600,000 just two or three years later?

Dollar cost averaging is an investment strategy based on the premise that no one can successfully time the market. Recognizing that stocks *can* fall sharply in value in a short period of time, many advisors recommend dollar cost averaging – investing at regular intervals over a long period.

If you are enrolled in a 401K or similar type of investment plan, you *are* practicing a default dollar cost averaging strategy. Reinvesting your <u>dividends</u> is another form; instead of receiving the dividend in cash, you reinvest it in shares of the paying company or <u>mutual fund</u>.

THE LESSON

No stock investment strategy is foolproof. If stock prices rise, you may regret that you didn't invest all of your $1 million immediately. But if stock prices subsequently decline, you will be happy you engaged in dollar cost averaging because the cost of your later investments will be at lower prices. You cannot successfully time the market. Trying to buy before stocks rise, or trying to sell them before they tank, is a fool's errand. Stay the course, ride the waves, and think long-term.

> *LONG TERM CONSISTENCY*
> *BEATS SHORT TERM INTENSITY.*
> *— Bruce Lee*

The underlying logic of dollar cost averaging can be found in many of our daily routines.

If you are serious about dieting, you consistently watch what you eat until you reach your desired weight. You are aware of the physical costs of yo-yo dieting and weight loss, and you control those costs.

If you are serious about running a marathon you train for it by following a consistent training protocol until your body says, "OK, now we can run 26.2 miles."

If you are serious obtaining a college degree, you commit to years of study (and *maybe* a little partying) until you have that diploma in hand.

If you are serious about keeping your car in safe, reliable condition, you follow a periodic maintenance schedule. True, you still might get a flat tire, but you won't beat yourself up for overlooking oil and filter changes.

Finally, if you are serious about building trust, and commitment with your spouse or partner, you don't show it twice a year on birthdays and anniversaries. You show it through long-term consistent behavior that says, "I care about you and will not violate your trust."

We can predict with 100-percent assurance that you will have good days and bad days while working toward your long-term goals, whatever they are. Consistency means putting forth the effort on the bad days just as you do on the good days.

Remember the parable of the tortoise and the hare. The hare was faster; but the tortoise, ever the consistent reptile, won the race.

EXPECTED RETURN

The expected rate of return is the rate of return you expect ... in the future. It is a likely rate, not a guaranteed rate. Because it isn't guaranteed, your actual rate of return could be higher or lower than what you originally expected.

The future is uncertain. Next year's interest rate, the level of next year's S&P 500 Index, the amount of rain that will fall on you next year, how much money you will have when you retire, the won-loss record of your favorite sports team next season, are all unknowns.

In each case, you may have an idea of the expected outcome. You can refer to the expected interest rate, the expected S&P 500 performance, how much rainfall will soak you to the skin and whether your team can manage a winning season. But the actual result in each case may be very different than what you expected.

There are two sources of the expected rate of return on an investment, a cash flow, such as a dividend, and an expected capital gain caused by expected price appreciation (or a capital loss caused by an expected price decline). Most of the uncertainty about your rate of return comes from the price change.

Investment analysts often offer their opinions on the stock market's expected rate of return. They are only guessing, even if they're doing it on television or in *The Wall Street Journal*.

THE LESSON

We expect many things in life. When it comes to stock investing, expectations are rarely met. The expected return is just one possible outcome, but not a guaranteed outcome. Imagine 100 flips of a coin. The expected number of heads (or tails) is 50. The actual number of heads may be quite different. Probability is based on a statistical analysis and estimation. Life is real, sometimes joyous, and sometimes heart breaking. You might expect a financial return, but that expectation is only based on the probabilities of many different possible outcomes. ♪

MY EXPECTATIONS WERE REDUCED TO ZERO WHEN I WAS 21. EVERYTHING SINCE THEN HAS BEEN A BONUS.
— Stephen Hawking

These are the five things you should expect when you're expecting a return:

1. You can expect to feel like you're on an emotional roller coaster. The highs and lows, elation and depression are the direct response to what you're hearing, reading and seeing. You've taken a risk and expect a certain return. As time passes, expectations of that risk are likely to change. You're coming to grips with the fact that the return you expect may not be so certain.

2. If you bought individual stocks or bonds through a broker, you can expect the broker will communicate with you differently when things go bad than when they go well. When things go bad, your broker will take longer to return your calls and emails. (Corporations do the same when reporting earnings; they delay bad news.) And when he finally does, he will likely talk about issues other than your investment. When things go well, not only will your broker return your calls quickly, he'll even suggest a few new investments.

3. You can expect to search for positive news when making your initial investment and change that search pattern the longer you stay invested. When you first buy, you have high expectations; otherwise, you wouldn't risk your money. You search for confirmation of your expectations. As conditions change, so too will your information search.

4. You can expect to feel smarter than you ought to feel when your expectations are exceeded, and dumber than you ought to feel when expectations fall short.

5. You can expect, if you lose money, that someone will tell you, "it's only money." Depending on how much you lost, those words won't necessarily make you feel any better.

Bottom line: Life is about managing expectations.

MARGIN

When you buy securities on margin, you are borrowing to make your purchase, increasing the total amount you invest. You cannot borrow everything; you must put up some of your own money (equity).

Margin refers to the percentage of your investment that is your money. Note that this definition differs from the concept of profit margin (a profitability ratio), which is the percentage profit on sales (net income/sales).

The Federal Reserve, which is the central bank in the United States, regulates the minimum margin percentage. Since 1974, the required initial margin when you first invest is 50 percent. If you have $10,000 to invest in stocks, you can borrow an additional $10,000 from your broker and invest a total of $20,000.

But what if you buy on margin and the value of your stocks declines? Your margin (equity/total value of your portfolio) will also decline. If you borrow $10,000 and put up $10,000 of your own money, a 50 percent decline in stock value causes you to lose 100 percent of your personal investment. A portfolio with 50 percent equity and 50 percent borrowed money will be twice as volatile as one with 100 percent equity.

All brokerage firms have a "maintenance margin requirement," which is applied after your initial investment. If your margin percentage falls to that level, you will receive a margin call from your broker, requiring you to deposit more money into your account. You will get a margin call before you lose everything. If you fail to put up more equity, your broker will sell some or all of your securities. When you buy on margin, your securities become collateral for the loan, and you will pay interest on that loan.

THE LESSON

We cannot stress enough the risk of buying on margin. If the values of stocks you own rise by more than the margin interest rate you are paying (these rates differ), you will be rewarded for buying on margin, and the rate of return you earn on your investment will increase. But if your stocks decline (as they have annually in 25 percent of all years since 1926), you may get a margin call. It may prove to be one of the worst financial nightmares you ever face. Thoroughly understand what you are getting into if you decide to buy on margin.

Mount Rushmore enshrines Presidents George Washington, Theodore Roosevelt, Abraham Lincoln and Thomas Jefferson. Imagine for a moment that we did the same for iconic investors – philanthropists. What faces would be on that mountain?

You can bet your portfolio that John Templeton would make a very short list of candidates. Consider this endorsement from *Money* magazine: John Templeton is "arguably the greatest global stock picker of the century." His philanthropy also had global impact.

So, when he says, "'This time is different' are the four most expensive words in the English language," we should heed his advice. But his advice extends beyond cautioning investors against believing that their current investments on margin will be more profitable than the last ones.

More broadly, his advice applies to how we live our lives and whether we change our behavior when changes must be made.

If you have unsuccessfully tried two diets and say the third will be different, you may or may not lose weight.

If you have broken two previous budgets and say the third is different, you may or may not become financially solvent.

Say "this time is different" only if *you* are different. If you haven't changed, neither will your outcome.

Desire to change, commitment to change and a plan for change are necessary, but not sufficient. What you need over and above desire and commitment is the courage for self-examination. What self-defeating behaviors are preventing you from changing?

Unless you pay the emotional price for that examination, your new attempt at change will be a repeat of your past attempts; this time will *not* be different. The price you pay will be more than money; you will lose self-worth.

When you decide to change again after previous unsuccessful attempts, ask yourself a simple question: Is this time *really different*?

PROFITABILITY RATIOS

Is a corporation's net income of $1 million good or bad? It depends – $1 million *compared to what?*

Evaluating financial performance requires comparing profits to other variables, thus creating "financial ratios." When one of the variables is a measure of earnings (from the firm's <u>income statement</u>), the ratio is called a "profitability ratio." Here are some common examples:

- Profit margin on sales: net income divided by sales revenues.
- Return on assets (ROA): often net income divided by the firm's total <u>assets</u> (reported on the firm's <u>balance sheet</u>).
- Return on equity (ROE): net income divided by the firm's accounting book value of equity (the latter is also from the balance sheet). Many regard this ratio as the most important profitability ratio. It measures how much profit the firm is earning per dollar of equity <u>capital</u> that was invested in the firm.
- Earnings per share (EPS): net income divided by the number of outstanding shares of common <u>stock</u>.
- Price-to-earnings ratio (PE): market capitalization (stock price times shares outstanding) divided by net income. A PE ratio measures how much investors are willing to pay (the stock price) for a dollar of net income. PE ratios often are used to categorize value stocks (low PE ratios) and growth stocks (high PE ratios).

THE LESSON

"Ratio analysis" is like reading a racing form. Investors analyze financial statements and compute ratios to analyze <u>liquidity</u>, <u>leverage</u>, <u>efficiency</u> and profitability. They compare a company's ratios over time (is profitability improving?) and they compare ratios across companies (is a company doing as well as its competitors?). From these ratios, investors guess whether the stock price is likely to rise. As an investor, you should be familiar with these profitability ratios and how to use them, just as a handicapper uses the information in the racing forms to guess which horse will win. If you buy or sell a business, these ratios will also come into play. Remember, ratios are computed using historical data; future performance is never guaranteed.

Compared to what? It's an intriguing question.

How much do you weigh? Compared to what? Step on a scale and look at the number. You will have an objective measure. But feeling overweight or underweight – believing you are too fat or thin – goes beyond the reading on the scale. It is based on comparing your weight to others.

How fast are you driving? Compared to what? Look at the speedometer. But the speedometer only displays a number, it doesn't tell you if you are moving too fast or slow, or just right. The speed limit signs and the traffic ahead, behind, and beside you provide the *comparative* data. Those comparisons tell you how fast or slow you are moving.

Eleanor Roosevelt is telling us that the *compared to what* question, when applied to personal growth and self-esteem, may be self-defeating at best, and devastating at worst.

We go through life assessing our self-worth and developing a self-concept by answering the *compared to what* question. Over time, those answers create a positive, sense of self or a negative one.

You will never have enough, and you will never be fulfilled if you compare yourself to people who you think are better, happier, and more fulfilled than you are.

If you truly want to become a heathier, happier person tomorrow, ask yourself these questions: Am I a better person today than yesterday? What must I do to be a better person tomorrow?

Stop thinking, *compared to what.* Start thinking, *compared to the person I could become.*

YIELD AND YIELD CURVE

Often, you will see the terms "yield" or "yield to maturity" when considering a <u>bond</u> or other fixed income debt security. The yield is a measure of the <u>rate of return</u> you will earn if you buy the security, and if the issuer (corporation, municipality, etc.) does not default. It is a "promised yield."

<u>Bond</u> yields differ for many reasons. The two most important are a) the time until the bond "matures," meaning until the amount of time until issuer has repaid all of the interest on the security and its principal, and b) the probability that the issuer will default.

If you plot the yields on treasury securities as a function of their time to maturity, you will get what is called the "yield curve." It is usually upward sloping, meaning you get higher yields for long-term bonds. Sometimes, the yield curve is flat. Less frequently, it is downward sloping, or inverted, which means that you get higher yields on short-term bonds than on long-term bonds.

An inverted yield curve is one of the most reliable signals of an impending <u>recession</u>. Every post-World War II recession was preceded by an inverted yield curve. But sometimes, the yield curve inverts and there is no recession (hence the saying, "the yield curve has predicted 10 out of the last eight recessions").

You should be compensated for bearing default <u>risk</u>, and *on average*, you are. The higher the probability of default, the lower the bond rating and the higher the bond's yield. Standard and Poor's (S&P) and Moody's are the two largest bond rating agencies. S&P rates investment-grade bonds as AAA (the highest quality), AA, A, and BBB. Riskier, high-yield (junk) bonds are rated as BB, B, CCC, CC, C (the lowest quality issue that has not defaulted). In October 2020, typical 20-year AAA, AA, A and BBB corporate bonds were yielding 2.16 percent, 2.34 percent, 2.59 percent, and 3.36 percent respectively.

THE LESSON

You should be rewarded for bearing risk, no matter the shape of the yield curve. Higher-yielding bonds are riskier. The best advice: Think of your planning horizon. If you have a long planning horizon, buy longer bonds. If your planning horizon is short, invest in shorter bonds. Because issuers of corporate bonds may default, DIVERSIFY across issuers and industries. Buy a high yield <u>mutual fund</u>, rather than the high-yield bonds of just one or two firms.

> *THE NOTION THAT A HUMAN BEING SHOULD*
> *BE CONSTANTLY HAPPY IS A UNIQUELY MODERN,*
> *UNIQUELY AMERICAN, UNIQUELY DESTRUCTIVE IDEA.*
> — *Andrew Weil*

The yield curve graphically illustrates the return rate of bonds projected over time – useful information indeed. It also depicts a reality that the yield curve is not constant over time. Rates may go up or down.

Investors understand that financial performance varies over time and are not surprised when it does. They may not be happy with the changes, but aside from drastic changes, they are not shocked. In fact, they factor time and risk into their decisions.

Andrew Weil, famous for advocating a holistic approach to healing and health, provides a parallel perspective about happiness. He tells us that being happy is not (and should not be) a perpetual state. Like financial yields, it changes over time.

More importantly, Weil is telling us that we fool ourselves if we expect to be constantly happy. Hmmm…. He wants us to consider that constant happiness is a "destructive idea."

But why is it destructive? Don't we deserve to be happy? Our life on this earth is limited and happiness is preferable to despair.

But the issue is not happiness; the issue is *constant* happiness.

If we expect to be constantly happy, we will necessarily set ourselves up for heartache and depression. Indeed, expecting to be constantly happy sets the stage for periods of unhappiness. We will experience emotional and physical trauma in our lives. Assuming we are immune from that trauma is to live in denial.

Happiness only has meaning because we have experienced despair and heartache, because we have risen from the depth of emotional pain. We have been to the valley and look forward to the mountain top.

Because the only constant in life is change, accept its highs and lows with resilience and hope, not dread and despair. If you do, happiness will be predictable but ever changing.

CHAPTER 3

FINANCIAL LITERACY FOR BORROWING AND LENDING

There are times in your life when you may borrow money and times when you may lend it. Indeed, if you use your credit cards for day-to-day purchases and buying a bank CD, you are both borrowing and lending at the same time. All of which falls under the general heading of "renting" money. You rent your own money when you lend it, and others rent it to you when you borrow. The interest rate is the price of the rental. The following yins and yangs highlight the essentials of wealth-building through borrowing and lending, showing you which paths to take and which to avoid when renting someone else's money or charging others to rent yours. Choosing the right path leads to financial gain without sacrificing heart and soul.

LEVERAGE

Leverage is a term usually used for borrowing. When you borrow, you "lever yourself up" or lever up your investments by using other peoples' money, rather than your own. Using your own money is called "equity." Equity reflects ownership.

Leverage creates risk for the investor/borrower. The range of outcomes, both good and bad, increases with the percentage of leverage you take on. Leverage requires that you go into debt. When you buy stock on margin, you are creating leverage.

Leverage creates an added cost: interest expense. If you fail to pay the interest or principal that is due, you may also risk default and be forced into bankruptcy. Lenders impose terms and requirements on the borrower to manage the risk of default. These include collateral, limits on dividends and restrictions on new investment.

Corporate leverage is created by fixed costs -- costs that a company must pay, regardless of its sales or output. It comes in two forms: operating leverage, created by the firm's fixed operating costs, and financial leverage, created by fixed financial costs such as interest expense.

Several ratios that measure corporate financial leverage are computed using financial statement data. Two common leverage ratios are the firm's debt-to-equity ratio and its debt-to-assets ratio.

THE LESSON

Leverage is beneficial when you can earn a rate of return on your investments higher than your borrowing cost. If you can borrow at 5 percent and manage to earn over 5 percent on your investments, then the debt will improve your results and you win. If you cannot earn 5 percent, you lose. Either way, leverage creates risk, so you should use leverage with caution. If you invest in stocks, understand how leverage increases your risk exposure. Profitability of highly levered companies, and hence their stock prices, will be more variable than similar relatively unleveraged companies.

> *GIVE ME A LEVER LONG ENOUGH AND A FULCRUM ON WHICH TO PLACE IT AND I SHALL MOVE THE WORLD.*
> *— Archimedes*

Leverage has a specific meaning to investors and bankers. It also has a meaning for engineers and physicists. Archimedes's lever is an application of that meaning. What these meanings have in common is producing an outcome by using levers to amplify force.

Leverage also significantly affects how you deal with others, and how you amplify forces in those dealings. In human relations, a lever is any social or psychological pressure you believe will help you achieve your goal.

When you are negotiating for something, you are constantly looking for levers that will move the other person to your position.

If you ever used a friend or relative to obtain a job, you were using leverage: pull, clout and influence.

If you ever tried to persuade someone by using peer pressure from others, you were using leverage: influence and pressure.

If you ever used recommendations from high-status friends to obtain a loan, you were using leverage: influence and advantage.

If you choose organizations to join based primarily on their status, prestige, and potential for networking, you are contemplating using future levers.

But just as leveraging entails risks in financial planning, so too are there risks when leveraging social and psychological pressure. The risk is what you might lose by applying pressure without thinking of the consequences.

Others might see you as manipulative, trying to gain an unfair advantage. They may also see you as unworthy of your status or attainment because you achieved it through unjust influence instead of merit.

Leveraging is human nature. When confronting obstacles we try to amplify forces. When you use levers to move others, make sure you are doing it with heart and soul and not diminishing their heart and soul. Otherwise, you will lose by winning.

THE FIVE Cs OF CREDIT

You've heard the lyric, "love makes the world go round." In person-to-person relationships, that may be true. In terms of commerce, however, credit makes the world go around.

Like love, credit is based on a trusting relationship between two parties: The lender provides a good, service or loan to the borrower without immediate payment, trusting that payment will be received in the future.

Terms for granting the credit typically take the form of a written agreement between borrower and lender, allowing for a possible legal remedy if the payment is not received.

When lenders decide whether to provide the credit, they take five factors into account. These factors, which assess the likelihood of repayment, each begin with the letter C. They are called the Five Cs of Credit:

Character: What evidence supports the potential debtor's trustworthiness, integrity and honesty? Credit score and personal recommendations are important considerations for this C.

Capacity: What is the potential debtor's ability to repay the loan? Work history, cash flow and physical health are important considerations.

Capital: What is the debtor's total net worth relative to the amount borrowed?

Collateral: What are the available assets to back up the loan? This C is more important for secured (collateralized) loans, (e.g., house, car) than for unsecured loans (e.g., credit card debt).

Conditions: What are the prevailing economic factors (inflation, interest rates, competition) affecting the decision?

THE LESSON

Both lenders and borrowers take a risk when agreeing to a loan. The lender's risk is that the loan may not be repaid, requiring time, energy, and possibly legal intervention. The borrower's risk is that unforeseen factors may prevent repayment, setting the stage for a long-term debt burden and possibly bankruptcy. Whether you are the lender or the borrower, understand the meaning and implications of the Five C's of Credit, and negotiate the loan accordingly.

Most people are overconfident; according to one study, 65 percent of all Americans think they are more intelligent than average. Richard Thaler, Nobel laureate in economics, provides an illuminating perspective on human nature generally, and the overconfidence bias specifically.

Apply Thaler's analysis to borrowing and lending. Although borrowers vary demographically, taking out loans for many different reasons, most have one thing in common. They are confident that they will pay it off. Otherwise, they would not sign the note. Unfortunately, they may be overconfident.

Lenders also see themselves as above average, believing they are not stupid enough to loan money to people who can't pay it back; they are confident in their ability to discern credit risk. After all, they call themselves "risk managers." Unfortunately, they too may be overconfident.

Name us one banker who would say, "I'm below average in assessing credit risk." You're probably smiling as you think about this question; you can't imagine a banker saying that. And if you happen to be a banker, then you're probably laughing out loud.

Time for a reality check: Optimism is an admirable way to live your life; having a positive outlook is more life-affirming than having a negative outlook. Confidence and a "can do" attitude will get you far in this world. But overconfidence is a sign of hubris, denial, and wishful thinking.

When it comes to decisions involving risk and potential loss, obtain as much objective data as possible and fight the temptation to see yourself as above average (unless, of course, you *are* demonstrably above average).

Finally, optimism tempered with realism will undoubtedly place you among those who truly are above average.

FICO SCORE

Want to know how much you weigh? Step on a scale. Want to know your heart rate? Count the beats per minute. Want to know if you are a good golfer? Count your total strokes over 18 holes. But if you want to know if you are a good credit risk, you will have to check your FICO score.

FICO is an acronym derived from Fair Isaac Corporation, the company that created the metric for assessing credit worthiness. It is the most widely used credit score – the "gold standard," according to auto dealers, mortgage lenders and credit card issuers. Scores range from 300-850. The lower the score, the greater the credit risk; the higher the score, the lower the risk. A score less than 600 is considered sub-prime, and thus questionable.

Your FICO score is based on an algorithm composed of five factors, which overlap the Five C's of Credit:

1. Payment history: Do you pay on time?

2. Current indebtedness: How must do you owe?

3. Type of current credit: House? Credit cards? Auto? Personal Loans?

4. Length of credit history: How long have you been receiving credit?

5. New accounts: How many and what type of new credits accounts have you recently opened?

Currently, many apps and other internet-based sources provide easily accessible FICO scores. If a lender is considering taking you on as a credit risk, you may assume that your score has been scrutinized.

THE LESSON

A FICO score is a measurement taken at a single point in time. That score can change as your credit history changes. If your score raises red flags (a score less than 500), set up a plan to raise it: pay off your debts, check reports for accuracy, close accounts at collection agencies, negotiate with current lenders. If you want to be seen as more creditworthy then do those things that will make you more worthy of credit. ♪

Do we need checklists and scores for making yes/no decisions? We sure do. Be thankful that pilots, surgeons, and air traffic controllers follow checklists, metrics and formal procedures. Otherwise, people would die.

And yes, even though there is a degree of subjectivity in computing FICO scores, applying them is a better option than simple guess work, especially if lenders don't have personal knowledge of borrowers.

But let's take another look at keeping a score.

We keep score in sporting events because that is the only way of knowing who won and who lost. But are relationships with friends and family a sport? Do we see our role in those relationships as winning or losing? Keeping score between and among friends or family, tallying emotional scars to get even, diminishes our soul and our humanity.

Think about your most satisfying and gratifying relationships. Neither you nor that person are perfect. There may have been inadvertent slights that troubled both of you, but neither of you kept score. You were both willing to forgive, forget and move on.

Now think about the most toxic, painful relationship. That relationship may not only be defined by emotional scars; it may also be defined by a get-even scorecard. If so, forgiveness and forgetting have been replaced by revenge and retribution.

If you're keeping a get-even score card, ask yourself if winning in that relationship is more important than what you might lose – the relationship itself. You incur significant cost in holding a grudge, a cost that diminishes your humanity and your potential for growth. Is that a cost you really want to pay?

AMORTIZATION

A loan is amortized when it is paid off over time with periodic (e.g., monthly) payments. Mortgages (loans to buy real estate) and auto loans are amortized. For both loans, you borrow money and make monthly payments. Each payment includes both principal (paying down, or amortizing, the loan) and interest (the dollar cost of borrowing the loan balance; it equals the interest rate times the loan balance).

Initial payments are mostly interest, and less principal. The final payments are mostly principal, and relatively little interest. When you take out a loan, you should receive an "amortization schedule," which states the relative split between interest and principal in each payment over time.

Suppose you borrow $200,000 to buy a house with no down payment. The interest rate is 4 percent; the loan is for 30 years with payments to be made monthly (360 monthly payments). This mortgage is amortized. Each monthly payment is $954.83. The first payment is $666.67 of interest and $288.16 of principal. So, after your first payment, you have paid off $288.16 of your loan; your equity in the house is $288.16, and you now owe just $199,711.84 to the lender. The last payment is $3.17 of interest and $951.66 of principal.

THE LESSON

Many loans are amortized. Others, such as credit card debt and corporate bonds, are not. Some mortgage loans, called interest-only mortgages, are also not amortized. The advantage of interest-only mortgages is that they have lower payments (only interest, no principal). But they have the disadvantage of not allowing you to build up equity in the house, which occurs as the original loan is amortized. When you borrow for a major purchase of a potential asset, we recommend that you amortize the loan; after you have made all the payments, you own the asset.

A lender expects payment. But sometimes the lender receives an excuse in lieu of payment. If you were the lender, how would you feel if a person offered you an excuse for nonperformance rather than delivering what you expected?

You're probably thinking, "It depends." Is the excuse justified? Is the excuse habitual behavior or is this excuse an exception? How much pain is this person's nonperformance costing me? Depending on answers to these questions, the excuse may or may not be excused.

We have all received excuses for nonperformance and because none of us is perfect, we've all offered our own excuses as well. Whether offering an excuse or judging an excuse, we should consider Alexander Pope's wisdom. Making excuses for nonperformance is a "loser's way out" and has long term personal costs – lost credibility and diminished personal growth.

Are there times and circumstances when an excuse is justified? There are, and most reasonable people getting an excuse under those conditions would understand. Similarly, many lenders will work with buyers who offer an excuse, along with an apology for nonperformance and a compensatory plan.

But excuses that are habitual speak more about character than about circumstances. If you ever get a chance to watch a marathon, notice that some of the competitors are in wheelchairs and some are running on one or two prosthetic limbs. Ask those marathoners what they think about excuses.

Work harder at fulfilling commitments than finding excuses for not fulfilling them.

APR

The APR (annual percentage rate) is an annual interest rate charged for borrowing money. Visit any credit card website, and you will see its APR listed. The interest rate on mortgages (loans to buy real estate) and auto loans are also expressed as APRs. The APR also may be used to indicate the annual rate of return earned on an investment such as a bank CD.

The APR takes an unannualized short term (e.g., weekly or monthly) percentage rate and annualizes it without compounding. This is sometimes called the "simple" method: you multiply the short-term (less than a year) unannualized interest rate by the number of periods during the year.

For example, if the short period of time is a month, you multiply the monthly interest rate by 12 because there are 12 months in a year; this is simple interest. You would multiply a weekly interest rate by 52.

Suppose you borrow $100 today, and at the end of the month, you are charged $1 in interest. The unannualized (monthly) interest rate is 1/100 = 1 percent. To compute the APR, you multiply the monthly interest rate by 12. The annual percentage rate is 12 percent. Note that often, fees and other charges are added to the interest when computing an APR.

There is a second method to annualize a short-term unannualized rate: with compounding. If interest earns interest (compounding), then the interest rate is called either APY (Annual Percentage Yield), or EAR (Effective Annual Rate). But don't be confused; APY and EAR are the same thing.

THE LESSON

If you are borrowing, try to get the lowest APR. If you are lending, try to get the highest APR. But keep in mind that the APR has a flaw: It fails to account for compounding interest (where interest earns interest). The true effective cost (of borrowing) and the true effective rate of return (if you are a lender) is higher than the APR. The true effective rate is the annual percentage yield (APY); also called the effective annual rate (EAR). It's better to compare APY's (EAR's) than it is to compare APR's. In the notes, we illustrate that there are times when borrowing at a lower (e.g., 12%) APR will actually cost you more than borrowing at a higher (e.g., 12.1%) APR. You should compare APY's because they provide your true borrowing rate. ♪

The older you get, the more you realize that life is a series of trade-offs and compromises. This realization is not cynical or nihilistic. It is an acceptance that we are not living in an idyllic, utopian world.

In that world all of us would be continually satisfied. Conflicts would be non-existent. Business would be conducted with smiles, promises, and handshakes instead of contracts, invoices and receipts.

But that world only exists in wishful thinking. In the real world promises, smiles and handshakes may not even suffice when family members loan money to one another.

The compromise and trade-offs between an honest, ethical lender and an honest, ethical borrower are relatively straightforward. Once we've decided to purchase something on credit, or once we've agreed to the terms of a credit card, we are necessarily committed to paying off the loan – with interest.

You agree to the terms in exchange for the freedom to purchase something now without the financial resources in hand to purchase it. The lender agrees to offer the credit in exchange for the "rent" you pay for that credit.

So, once you accept the reality of this trade-off, and agree to the terms of that trade, you should move forward, envisioning a clean credit record. However, accepting the credit terms without accepting the reality of the trade-off is living in a world of your own making.

You can't have it both ways. Don't accept the terms if you don't accept the trade-off. Peter Ustinov accepted the trade-off. You should, too. Accept the reality, move on, and flourish.

ARM

An ARM is an adjustable rate <u>mortgage</u>. A mortgage is a loan to buy real estate such as a house. When you borrow money, the price you pay is called the interest rate, which is a percentage of the loan amount that you must periodically pay to the lender for "renting" the money.

Because an ARM is "adjustable," the interest rate will periodically change. Many ARMs adjust the interest rate annually, once every three years or once every five years. An ARM differs from a fixed rate mortgage, which has a fixed, or constant, interest rate over the entire term of the mortgage loan.

Usually, the interest rate will be set and/or adjusted according to a formula linked to a benchmark index. For example, maybe the interest rate will change depending on whether three-month treasury bill interest rates rise or fall. Or depending on how 10-year treasury note interest rates change. Or maybe the adjustment will depend on changes in an index of mortgage rates.

THE LESSON

Four lessons:

1) You may face the fixed-versus-variable interest rate decision many times in your life. Your decision will depend on whether you are a borrower or a lender (investor), and whether you believe interest rates will rise or fall.

2) If you think interest rates are going to fall over the term of the loan, consider an adjustable rate if you are borrowing money. Also lock up a fixed long-term interest rate on investments you make.

3) If you think interest rates will rise in the future, then lock in a fixed rate mortgage today; as a lender, lend for only short periods of time (effectively making it a variable rate loan), and enjoy a higher <u>rate of return</u> as interest rates rise.

4) If you have no idea what interest rates will do, then don't speculate; lock in a borrowing rate or lending rate for your specific planning horizon. Remember, if you have a long-term fixed-rate mortgage, you can usually <u>refinance</u> the loan if interest rates fall. However, you will have to consider refinancing fees if you do.

Total control is both wishful thinking and doomed thinking. Yet even though total control is beyond anyone's reach, intelligent and manageable control is achievable.

The first step towards manageable control is to humbly accept that because of an ever-changing world, we do not have total control. To survive and succeed, we must critically consider options and the consequences of those options.

Start with critically looking at yourself.

Are you a victim of fate or an agent of fate? This crucial question and your answer will forever determine your future success and your emotional well-being. Victims are more likely than agents to be angry, depressed, and unforgiving. They are also more likely to see themselves as martyrs and losers.

We have the potential to make decisions today that will affect our lives tomorrow. We have the potential for self-reflection, critical thinking, and personal empowerment. We can choose to become the agent of our own fate.

If our current situation is intolerable, we need not accept it. We can transform the intolerable and improve our fate. Once you understand the difference between controlling life's forces versus controlling the self, you become empowered and will increase self-reflection and critical thinking.

For example, taking on long-term debt and weighing the financing options for that debt, is an example of critically considering options and consequences. Signing the loan agreement is a personal testament that you are not a victim but an empowered decision-maker.

You clarified your goals, considered your options, and are fully aware of the consequences of your decision. In the absence of those critical considerations, life will control you, and you will feel like a victim, not a victor.

Finally, if you hate your mortgage more than you love your house, don't blame the lender or your real estate agent. They presented options. You made the decision.

COLLATERAL

If you borrow money, the lender will likely require collateral. Collateral is any asset that can, if the lender agrees, serve as security for the loan. In pledging collateral, the borrower agrees that the lender may legally seize the asset in the event of default (i.e., the borrower fails to repay the loan).

Collateral is motivating for both a lender and a borrower. A borrower is motivated to pay the loan for fear of losing the asset. A lender is motivated to provide the funds because an asset is available in the event of default. Collateral is often the make-or-break issue in securing a loan.

If you borrow to buy a car, the car is collateral for the auto loan. If you borrow (a mortgage) to buy a house, the real estate is collateral for the mortgage. If you borrow to buy stocks (buying on margin), then the securities in your investment account serve as collateral for the loan. If you take out a personal loan, the lender may require you to pledge personal items as collateral. In that case, the collateral and its value are likely to be negotiated.

The interest you pay on a loan is affected by the value of the collateral you pledge. The greater the value of the collateral, the more leverage you have for negotiating the interest rate.

Corporations issue bonds when they borrow money from investors; they may even pledge collateral for some of their bonds (e.g., "mortgage bonds"), while other bonds, called "debentures," are unsecured.

Often, the lender will have a lien against the collateral, which means that the lender has the legal right to seize the collateral, should the borrower default. While the loan still exists, the borrower cannot sell the collateral without the approval of the lien holder.

THE LESSON

When requesting a loan, be prepared to offer collateral, even if the loan is from a friend or relative. Your offer of collateral is a sign of good faith. A loan that is not backed by collateral is called an unsecured loan, usually backed by the credit history of the borrower. Your character and payment history could be collateral depending on your relationship with the lender. Whether you are the lender or the borrower, make sure there are no other liens on the collateral.

We defined collateral in financial terms: something you are willing to lose in exchange for what you expect to gain. But consider collateral in human terms. When you put up collateral for a loan, you are making a bet with yourself. The heart and soul of collateral is the negotiation with yourself, not with the lender.

This is the essence of your personal bet: You believe the collateral you are willing to lose will not be lost because the loan will be paid. You also believe that, in the unlikely event you default and lose the collateral, that loss would have been worth it given what you hoped to gain.

We all have heard stories of companies started by founders mortgaging their house, or putting other "skin in the game." Yes, those would-be entrepreneurs negotiated with lenders; but they ultimately made bets with themselves. To paraphrase Csonka, they were willing to lose to win.

Finally, recognize that if you have a family, they too may have skin in the game, taking risks not of their own choosing. Whenever you ask a spouse or children to bear personal sacrifices because of your financial decisions, you may be creating *collateral damage.*

The heart and soul of collateral and collateral damage: Consider the potential losses in time, energy, focus and stress you and your loved ones may incur whenever you make that financial bet.

MORTGAGES

A mortgage is a loan to buy your home or other piece of real estate. The property you buy serves as <u>collateral</u> for the loan. If you make all of your monthly mortgage payments, you will pay off your loan and own your property, free and clear.

When you buy a home, you will have to decide between a fixed-rate mortgage or an adjustable rate mortgage (<u>ARM</u>). You will also have to decide on the term of the loan, typically 15 or 30 years.

If you fail to make a payment, immediately talk to your lender or HUD-approved counselor. You want to avoid <u>foreclosure</u>, which means you will be evicted, and the lender will take control of what was your property. Request <u>forbearance</u>.

If you are 62, with sufficient equity in your home, and you need cash, you may qualify for a reverse mortgage – borrowing against the equity you have in your home. You immediately get your cash and make no payments on the reverse mortgage loan. Instead, each month the amount you owe on your home goes up. When you sell your home, you (or your heirs) repay the loan.

Examine all your options before taking out a reverse mortgage loan, such as <u>refinancing</u> your existing mortgage. If you take out a reverse mortgage, you have three days to cancel it in writing; this is called "rescission."

THE LESSON

Buying a home is a significant investment, financially and emotionally. It is also a proven strategy for building <u>wealth</u>. But before buying, answer three questions: 1) Is there a reasonable chance you will live in the house for five or more years? 2) Are your after-tax monthly ownership costs affordable, and comparable to your monthly rental costs? Ownership costs include interest, principal, <u>insurance</u>, property taxes and reasonable monthly maintenance. We say "after-tax" because some homeowners will find it advantageous to deduct the interest and property taxes on their home. 3) Can you afford a 20-percent down payment? If you can answer yes to all three questions, we recommend you buy what could become your major <u>asset</u>.

> *SWEAT EQUITY IS THE MOST*
> *VALUABLE EQUITY THERE IS.*
> — Mark Cuban

"HOORAY! We've paid off the mortgage."

Whenever you hear someone say that, you are looking at a person with a huge grin. Some people even host parties celebrating final mortgage payments. And rightly so. Paying off a mortgage is a celebration of a multi-year journey that began with a dream and ended with home ownership and equity.

That equity provides both security and options. The security means you have a home free and clear, and no longer have to worry about making a monthly payment. The option means you may be able to use the house as a "piggy bank" if you decided to draw down that equity.

But there is another type of equity providing security and options: sweat equity.

When you pay off your mortgage, you benefit from years of focus, commitment, budgeting, sacrifices and labor – the things that make up sweat equity. You earned the money, and then made the commitment to use that hard-earned money for a house, rather than for other things.

The security of your sweat equity is a sense of pride and accomplishment. You have the psychological security of knowing you are capable and competent. You did it. You made it happen; you paid off a mortgage. You proved to yourself and others that you could follow through on a major commitment. You passed your test.

That sense of competence and confidence also provides options. Just as financial equity in your house enables you to use that money for other pursuits, the confidence and competence resulting from sweat equity empowers other pursuits.

When you make that final mortgage payment, raise a toast to your sweat equity – the heart, soul, tears and commitment that made it happen.

If you have a mortgage, look forward to the day when you too will say, "HOORAY! We've paid off the mortgage."

REFINANCE

Interest rates may fall after you finance a home <u>mortgage</u>. However, the good news is that if that happens, you may be able to refinance your loan and come out ahead. You borrow at the new, lower interest rate, paying off your existing loan. Like all <u>options,</u> the refinancing option has value.

However, your lender will charge several fees, known as refinancing costs. The monthly savings on your payments must be sufficiently high to compensate for those costs.

For example, suppose you borrow $300,000 for 30 years at 5 percent. Your monthly payment will be $1,610. Suppose that 10 years later, the interest rate is 4 percent. You will still owe $244,025 on your house (see <u>amortization</u>). If you refinance your loan balance of $244,025 (no equity is withdrawn) for 20 years because you have 20 years remaining on your old loan (you are *not* extending the life of your loan), then your new monthly payment will be $1,479, which is a $131/month savings. If your refinancing costs are less than $1,572, then this is a good deal because the closing costs will be recouped in under a year.

There are other issues to consider when refinancing a mortgage. You will have to decide whether to extend the life of your loan, if you want to withdraw some of your equity in the house, and how long you will likely live in your house. Taxes and whether you are deducting interest payments also play a role. These decisions make the financing an issue of relative tradeoffs.

THE LESSON

In general, you should not even think about refinancing unless you can reduce your interest rate by 1 percent or more. Consider refinancing if you can recoup your refinancing costs in one or two years. If you plan on living in your house for five or more years, then a three-year break-even loan may make sense. If a 15-year mortgage has a much lower interest rate than a 30-year mortgage, and if you can afford the higher payments, consider that 15-year mortgage; you will pay a lot less interest over the life of your loan.

> *YOU CAN'T GO BACK AND CHANGE THE BEGINNING, BUT YOU CAN START WHERE YOU ARE AND CHANGE THE ENDING.*
> — C. S. Lewis

We all have the option of how we will move forward: we do not have the option of changing the past. Refinancing is a powerful example of the impossibility of going back in time to change where you are now, but rather changing where you are now to create a better outcome tomorrow. The past is fixed; the future is yet to come. We cannot do over, but we can re-do.

We go through life not as perfect beings, but as human beings. Human frailty is the norm, not the exception. We all make mistakes, either by commission or omission. We all wish we had not done something we did, or not said something we said. We all wish there is something we should have done.

We all have regrets. Regret is painful, but it need not be paralyzing. Lewis's quote tells us that regret can be the impetus for making life-altering positive changes.

Regardless whether our mistake was one of omission or commission, we may find the decision we originally made is still not the best decision today. Circumstances change and a better option may present itself. When you have that option, take it.

To mitigate a life of regret, change today.

If you have hurt someone – intentionally or unintentionally – apologize. Whoever you hurt may or may not forgive and forget; that is their choice. Your choice is to accept responsibility for your past behavior and, more importantly, acknowledge that responsibility to those affected by it.

Keep an open mind. Opportunities and options are only available if you see them.

Finally, second chances will always exist. Tomorrow is a new day, a day of opportunity, hope, and second chances.

CHAPTER 4

FINANCIAL LITERACY
FOR LAW AND LEGACY

Financial transactions typically involve legal considerations, often affecting multiple parties. These considerations come into play when investing, borrowing, or lending. They are also significant at the end of your life. What legal issues should you consider when managing your money generally, and addressing end-of-life issues specifically? The yins and yangs that follow will help you answer this question so that your decisions in building your portfolio and bequeathing it will be lawful while reflecting heart and soul. ♪

FINANCIAL ADVISORS

We use the terms financial advisor, financial planner, wealth advisor and wealth manager interchangeably. Individuals with these titles may help with your spending, budgeting, and borrowing. They may also advise you on savings and investment decisions and create a plan to meet your long-term goals. Some only recommend an investment strategy while others actually make the investments for you (be sure these individuals are <u>fiduciaries</u>). Some will also help with your taxes, retirement, estate planning and <u>insurance</u> needs, and may even provide personal coaching and family therapy.

If you have less than $10,000 to invest and need help with your <u>asset allocation</u>, you might consider a "robo-advisor," an automated financial advisor. Be sure it only recommends <u>mutual funds</u> and <u>exchange traded funds (ETFs)</u> with low-expense ratios, and you feel comfortable with its recommendations. Robo-advisors are cheap, but you often get what you pay for.

While a degree in <u>finance</u>, accounting or economics is helpful, we know many successful advisors with liberal arts degrees. Search for a financial advisor with a professional credential such as the CFA® (Chartered Financial Analyst), CFP® (Certified Financial Planner), or PFS (CPA/Personal Financial Specialist). They met rigorous education and examination criteria to receive these credentials, are required to uphold ethical standards, and will suffer severe consequences if they don't.

If your financial advisor lacks these credentials, but you are happy with her, don't fix what ain't broke. There are many excellent and trustworthy financial advisors without these credentials, and we would trust them to manage our money in an instant.

Understand your advisor's compensation. Some are paid by the hour, while others get a percentage of <u>assets</u> under management (AUM); these are "fee-only" advisors. In general, we don't think you should pay more than 1 percent of AUM. Be wary if you are also paying commissions when you trade securities.

THE LESSON

Individuals in the investments field are highly regulated. But even with all the laws and regulations, *caveat emptor* (let the buyer beware). Be sure to read your advisor's Form CRS (Client Relationship Summary) or the form CRS of any advisor you are considering. The SEC explains how to use Form CRS at https://www.investor.gov/CRS. Take your time to choose and interview several advisors. You may be putting your financial life in that person's hands. ♪

> ## *TO ACHIEVE GREAT THINGS, TWO THINGS ARE NEEDED: A PLAN AND NOT QUITE ENOUGH TIME.*
> ## *— Leonard Bernstein*

At first glance, Leonard Bernstein's advice seems crazy. Intuitively, we assume we need sufficient time to achieve our goals. Also, workshops on planning and goal setting, and college courses on management emphasize the importance of time management.

Why then would this world-renown conductor tell the world we should have "not quite enough time?"

The answer is Bernstein lived and thrived with complexity and shifting demands. Because of his amazingly frenetic schedule as a lecturer, conductor, composer, TV personality, husband and father, his plans were constantly tested and compromised by unforeseen events. But regardless of the complexity and uncertainty, his reputation demanded he do great things.

Management consultants would concur that he was living proof that plans are important, but execution is paramount.

But there is another spark of genius in his advice: If you don't have "quite enough time" you are likely to operate with increased motivation. You know you must get it done and want to get it done. So you will do whatever it takes to get it done. You kick in another gear. You do it now!

A financial advisor provides advice. She tells you what to do. You must do it. It's your money and it's your life. You choose whether to kick it in gear.

Achieving *Your Total Wealth* requires balancing and blending financial goals with personal and family goals. There may not be "quite enough time" to do both. Find a way to do it anyway. Get it done!

FIDUCIARY

A fiduciary is an individual or company working on behalf of another individual (called the beneficiary or principal), who often manages that person's financial assets. You usually delegate to a fiduciary the ability to make trades and investment decisions for you.

A fiduciary is held to a very high standard, both ethically and legally, to work in the best interests of the other party. That's how conflicts of interest and the agency problem are controlled.

There are many other types of fiduciaries besides those who manage financial wealth. If you name a trusted individual to serve as the executor of your will, that person is expected to serve as a fiduciary. If you hire a lawyer, she is expected to serve as a fiduciary. Members of corporate boards of directors have a fiduciary duty to work only in the best interests of the company and its stockholders, not in their own self-interests.

There can be serious consequences if fiduciaries fail to fulfill their duty. Think of what you expect when you ask someone to be your fiduciary. Not only must she do her best for you, but she is also expected to be knowledgeable about you, your needs, laws, customs, and the changing market. She also should be transparent, trustworthy, honest and loyal.

THE LESSON

Ask your financial advisor if she also works for you as a fiduciary; get her answer in writing. If you are letting someone invest for you, she should be a fiduciary. Not all financial advisors are fiduciaries. Brokers and insurance agents are required to satisfy a lower standard than fiduciary duty, called the "suitability standard." However, the Securities and Exchange Commission (SEC) regulates all registered investment advisors (RIAs) as fiduciaries. All else equal, having your financial advisor adhere to a fiduciary standard is best, if you want the law on your side.

> *I WILL ABSTAIN FROM ALL INTENTIONAL WRONG-DOING AND HARM.*
> — *Excerpt of Hippocratic Oath*

When you are being treated by a physician, you assume he will diagnose and treat you to the best of his ability and not intentionally harm you. Similarly, you expect a fiduciary acting in your behalf will intentionally do no harm. We necessarily expect and deserve a "first do no harm" approach from those professionals. After all, we are risking our health *and* our wealth.

But suppose you had that same expectation of family, friends, and acquaintances. Suppose they had that same expectation of you. Imagine a "first do no harm" guiding principle for our behavior. Would your relationships with others be any different than they are today?

Indeed they would, and in significant ways.

Perhaps the most significant difference would be you and others would behave according to the Golden Rule: *Do unto others as you would have them do unto you*, has considerable overlap with first do no harm ethic.

We all want to be respected and appreciated. When we choose to trust someone, we want and expect that trust to be validated. We don't want to be cheated, conned, manipulated or selfishly used by anyone.

We want them to "abstain from all intentional wrong-doing and harm" when relating to us, and they want the same from us.

Will there be times when others hurt us and times when we hurt others? Sadly, yes. But if those wounds are truly unintentional, and if the motive was to help rather than hurt, we would understand and be living the Golden Rule.

We would also forgive and forget because that is what we would want from others.

The heart and soul of relating to others: abstain from all intentional harm.

FINANCIAL FRAUD

Even with regulation and constant reminders of *caveat emptor*, there is still considerable fraud and unethical behavior in investments and financial markets. Here are some of the most common frauds:

- *Bait and Switch:* Advertising or a price and selling at a higher price; selling an inferior product than the one advertised. *"Sorry, the advertised one is not in stock."* Sound familiar?
- *Ponzi Scheme:* Think Bernie Madoff. Providing returns to investors from funds provided by other investors.
- *Fraudulent Intimidation*: Obtaining payments over the phone because you are threatened by thieves purporting to be the FBI, IRS, Social Security or your local utility.
- <u>Foreclosure</u> *Relief Scams:* Fraudulent promises to save your home from foreclosure. You will lose the money you send them *and* your home.
- *Fraudulent Corporate Reporting:* Creating smoke and mirrors with accounting data. Think Enron, WorldCom, Theranos.
- *Churning Your Portfolio:* Unscrupulous financial advisors may churn (over-trade) their customers' accounts to generate commission revenue for themselves. Think <u>agency problem</u>.
- *Pump and Dump:* The fraudster first buys many shares of a <u>stock</u>, then releases false bullish statements and strong buy recommendations about it. As naïve investors pile into the stock, its price increases. The fraudster then unloads his shares at a profit, and your shares then plummet in value.
- <u>Fiduciary</u> *Fraud:* The person you trusted with your finances lied, cheated or stole.
- *Identity Theft:* If you don't protect your personal information, a virtual clone could place you in agonizing debt and legal jeopardy.

THE LESSON

If someone offers you a deal that sounds too good to be true, *run!* If Treasury securities and insured CDs are paying 2 percent and someone offers you a <u>risk</u>-free 10-percent <u>rate of return</u>, *run!* Understand what you are investing in; if you don't, then don't invest. Know who you are investing with; examine their experience, knowledge, credentials, licenses and motives. Never buy anything over the phone from a telemarketer without receiving a written proposal first. Guard your social security number with your life. Finally, nothing in the marketplace is free. ♪

> *THE LAST THING I WOULD HAVE EVER EXPECTED*
> *TO HAPPEN TO ME IN MY LIFE WOULD BE THAT IN*
> *FACT I WOULD BE ACCUSED OF DOING SOMETHING*
> *WRONG AND MAYBE EVEN SOMETHING CRIMINAL.*
> — Ken Lay

The question is not why evil people do evil things, but why good people do evil things.

Ken Lay, the founder of Enron, and a convicted felon, captures the disbelief and shock good people experience when confronted by their immoral or illegal acts. Good people, unlike bad people, are surprised by their actions and genuinely express remorse and guilt.

Good people see themselves following a virtuous path; deviating from it is the last thing they would have expected.

So why did it happen?

Psychological research suggests two reasons why the Ken Lays of the world find themselves agonizing over things they never thought they would do:

Need and Opportunity

There is no consistent demographic profile of the employee who steals. The strongest predictors of embezzlement are a) the employee needed the money, and b) the employee had opportunity and access. Need and opportunity go a long way in explaining why good people do bad things.

Slippery Slope

The most common metaphor for describing why good people do bad things is they took the first step down the slippery slope. They may feel remorse for the first time they lied , but the more they do it, the easier it becomes to rationalize. They have taken that first step down the slope and they start sliding.

Don't be surprised by evil acts performed by evil people. That is predictable. Unfortunately, evil acts performed by good people are not as predictable but are understandable.

Fraudulent acts are always a choice, but not an inevitable choice. For your sake, be wary of the slippery slope, and don't allow the temptation to cheat or lie rob you of your heart and soul.

LIVING WILL AND POWER OF ATTORNEY

If you are completing a questionnaire for an upcoming medical procedure, you will be asked many questions:

"Do you have a living will?"

"Have you designated a power of attorney?"

You will even be asked those questions when meeting with an estate planner for the first time.

Similarly, if you are unable to communicate, or are being treated at hospital, a friend or family member could be asked these questions.

A living will is a formal document specifying your wishes regarding medical treatment for prolonging life. It removes heart-wrenching decisions physicians and family members must make if you can't.

A power of attorney document moves beyond health care concerns *per se*. It designates someone to make decisions on your behalf regarding your long-term care, personal finances, and any legal issues that may arise.

In essence, a living will address questions related to prolonging life; power of attorney addresses questions related to issues while you are alive, which you cannot handle yourself due to incapacitation.

Finally, make sure the person you entrust with your power of attorney, is totally dedicated to act on your behalf and is not motivated by personal enrichment (see the Agency Problem).

THE LESSON

Loved ones should not have to agonize whether you want to survive on life support. Physicians should not have to decide whether DNR (Do Not Resuscitate) should be listed in your medical file. Similarly, you should have peace of mind, knowing that your personal care and finances will be managed according to your wishes. Communicate your decision regarding a living will and power of attorney to someone you trust and make sure the documents can be *easily* accessed. If your estate planner does not ask you about long term care insurance, your living will, or power of attorney, get a new planner.

> *IF WE LOSE LOVE AND SELF-RESPECT FOR EACH OTHER, THIS IS HOW WE FINALLY DIE.*
> — *Maya Angelou*

A living will and power of attorney represent not only medical, legal, and financial considerations, but love and self-respect as well. Family and friends who initiate end-of-life discussions undoubtedly do so with pain in their heart. Yet they overcome that pain because of their love and respect for that person.

Sometimes a doctor, nurse or chaplain initiates the discussion with the patient, family, or friends. Whether initiated by a medical professional or clergy, the discussion is necessarily emotional, requiring both courage and tact.

Reality is indeed painful. But discussing a living will openly, honestly and compassionately is cathartic for everyone. It can even be life-affirming.

Similarly, even though discussions about power of attorney can be couched in dry legal and financial terms, they can also be done with love and respect. Power of attorney is not a soulless abdication of decision-making. It is, in a sense, a "promissory note" that the long-term care and financial management will be handled with care and dignity.

Heart and soul are requisite if you are power of attorney, or if you initiate end of life discussion.

Maya Angelou reminds us that dying is defined not only by the absence of heart beats, but also by the presence of heart aches. A long life, void of love and respect, may be one way of defining "early death."

But you are not dead. Make your decisions, talk to loved ones and care givers about your decisions. Couch that conversation in love and respect, a true testament to life!

GUARANTOR VERSUS CO-SIGNER

Your son – let's call him Jack – has taken a job out of town, and he's found the "perfect" apartment. After seeing pictures of the place, you agree with him. That's the good news.

The bad news is that Jack's landlord, wanting to reduce *his* risk, has asked for a guarantor or a co-signer on the lease. Jack calls you, describing the situation. "Will you help me out?" he asks. "Don't worry, I'll pay the rent." What do you do?

Assuming you are willing to help Jack get the apartment, the first thing you should do is understand the difference between a co-signer and a guarantor, and the risks associated with each.

If you co-sign the lease for the apartment, you, too, are considered a tenant, even if you don't live there. As a tenant, you are liable for the rent, and any other conditions specified in the lease. If Jack's job doesn't work – if he is laid off or quits – and can't pay the monthly rent, the landlord and the courts will hold *you* contractually obligated. The advantage of co-signing is that since you are considered a co-renter, you do have the right to use the property if necessary.

If you agree in writing to be a guarantor, you are not considered a tenant. However, you still are at risk if Jack can't make his rent payment. In this case, though, as a guarantor, you are viewed as the payer of last resort; the landlord must exhaust all legal remedies for securing rent from tenants (Jack and co-signers) before securing payment from a guarantor. While being a payer of last resort sounds safe, you still ultimately have full financial responsibility with no rights to use the property.

THE LESSON

Being a co-signer or a guarantor on a legally binding contract means that you are subject to the relevant laws governing the agreement. These contracts may not involve real estate. They may concern transactions for a car, a student loan, or a personal loan. Love, friendship, and family commitment are undoubtedly at play when we assume financial risk for one another's contractual obligations. Unfortunately, the courts are justifiably required to follow the law, regardless of your emotional bonds. Co-signing or guaranteeing a contract is your choice. Both parties should understand the financial and relationship risks and returns.

> *BY AND LARGE, LIFE WILL GIVE YOU*
> *WHAT YOU DESERVE, AND IT DOESN'T*
> *GIVE A DAMN WHAT YOU LIKE.*
> — Ray Dalio

If life were fair, the good guys would always win and the bad guys would always lose. If life were fair, we would never get hurt; our trust in family and friends would never be violated. We would gladly agree to co-sign or guarantee another's legal obligation without a second thought.

But Dalio is not a cynic: He's a realist, and he's right: "Life doesn't give a damn what you like."

He's also right in asserting that "by and large, life will give you what you deserve." Helping others is a noble and praiseworthy way to live your life. Assistance, financial and otherwise, is good for the soul, especially if your motives are beneficent.

But cutting your neighbor's grass, baking cookies for a sick friend, checking on your neighbor's house while she is on vacation are all far different than assuming another person's financial risk. If you take on financial risk without due diligence, and the primary lender defaults, you will get what you deserve: a heartbreaking lesson about the fairness of life.

The concept of "fairness" has multiple meanings: legal, financial, and ethical. If you want to be treated fairly as a co-signer or guarantor, have honest, candid discussions about these multiple meanings.

Finally, if a friend or relative agreed to be your co-signer, go above and beyond in paying back the debt. They went out of their way for you. Do the same for them. When you do, you will also be following the advice from Warren Buffett's partner, Charlie Munger, "When you borrow a man's car, always return it with a tank of gas."

Following that advice will make life seem a little fairer.

EARNEST MONEY VERSUS SECURITY DEPOSIT

We all need a roof over our head. Some of us buy that roof, others rent it. Regardless of your intent to buy or rent, you will be expected to provide money during the initial negotiations. If you are a buyer, you will offer "earnest money." If you are a renter, you will put up a "security deposit."

Consider the following synonyms for earnest: serious, committed, dedicated, sincere. A seller wants and deserves to know that a potential buyer is committed, dedicated and sincere. Conversely, a buyer must demonstrate seriousness, commitment, sincerity and dedication to the buyer. Earnest money provides that earnestness; it represents good faith.

That money is provided in a check typically held in <u>escrow</u> until the final closing and may vary from 1 to 5 percent of the purchase price. At the time of closing, that good faith deposit is applied to the final purchase. But it is possible that if the buyer changes his mind, the seller will keep the earnest money.

A security deposit also represents good faith. But it is between a renter and a landlord. And, it goes further than earnest money. A security deposit is <u>insurance</u> for any damage to the property while the renter lives there. Security deposits are negotiable, but typically represent one month's rent. State laws vary regarding whether deposits earn interest, and when they have to be returned to the renter.

THE LESSON

We all know there is a difference between talking the talk and walking the talk. In real estate transactions, whether buying or renting, good faith money is "walking the talk." Finally, realize that good faith applies to both sides of the transaction. Buyers and sellers must operate on "good faith." So must renters and landlords. Absence of good faith opens the door for anger, acrimony, and potential litigation. Regardless which side of the transaction you are on, you should operate with good faith and with knowledge of the appropriate regulations.

> *DON'T MARRY THE PERSON YOU THINK YOU CAN LIVE WITH; MARRY ONLY THE INDIVIDUAL YOU THINK YOU CAN'T LIVE WITHOUT.*
> — James C. Dobson

Most of us go through life thinking and believing that we are good people, honoring our commitments, worthy of trust, and operating with good faith. We also like to believe that others also operate with good faith.

But there are dishonest, devious, untrustworthy people, and there always will be. Good faith is virtuous, but not a virtue shared by all. Philosophers and theologians have told us why virtuous behavior is common, but not universal...the disconnect between intent vs. behavior.

The essence of good faith is the commitment to do good, wanting to do what's right. When we are committed, we follow through on our promises. We have no trouble talking the talk or telling others how they should walk their talk. The trouble is commitment: actually walking the talk.

Dobson's quote helps us understand why good faith often results in unfulfilled promises. We may be earnest but are not committed. Being earnest simply means you want to do something; being committed means you will do it and are doing it.

When we commit we don't settle for second best; we reach for what we truly want and find a way to make it happen.

Not all engagement rings result in matrimony. (Some are even the basis of lawsuits.) Not all marriage vows, which are simply verbal commitments, result in lifelong bliss. Indeed, they are often disavowed in a courtroom. Similarly, not all real estate transactions are mutually rewarding for the parties involved, reflecting a breaking of promises and good faith.

If life teaches you anything, it teaches you that a promise of commitment is not a commitment. Good faith, in the absence of confirming behavior, is hypocritical at best and potentially illegal at worst.

The choice is yours: being earnest and trying to succeed or committing and succeeding.

BENEFICIARY

A beneficiary is an individual or entity designated to receive the distributions from your will, <u>insurance</u> policy, bank account or investment/securities account. Individual beneficiaries can be family - immediate or extended, or close friends. Organizational beneficiaries are charities, educational institutions, clubs, trusts, or combinations of them. If you are naming beneficiaries, you are called the benefactor.

When you create a will, policy or account, you will be asked to name a primary beneficiary, the individual or entity that is first in line to inherit your <u>assets</u> if you die, and a contingent beneficiary, who is second in line in case the primary beneficiary cannot be found or is no longer alive.

If you don't name a beneficiary, your assets will go into probate, a legal process which is costly, time-consuming and often contentious depending on the parties involved. When there are no beneficiaries, distribution of an estate's <u>assets</u> are governed by the laws of that state. Your heirs will be predictably distraught if you die without naming beneficiaries. It is also quite possible that some of them will be distraught if you *do* name beneficiaries.

THE LESSON

If you have assets, you will undoubtedly want to determine who gets them when you die. Naming beneficiaries for each of your bank accounts, investment accounts and insurance policies is thus essential. Review and update your beneficiaries regularly on all your accounts, policies and will. Perhaps you recently married or divorced, had children or changed your views on your favorite charities. Possibly tax laws have changed, affecting your beneficiary decisions. When naming beneficiaries in your will, consult a lawyer. Also talk to your personal <u>financial planner</u> about your beneficiaries. If you have considerable household assets (art, furniture, jewelry, heirlooms), create an inventory and specify their distribution in your will.

> *ONE OF THE THINGS THAT HAPPEN WHEN PEOPLE MAKE THE LEAP FROM A CERTAIN AMOUNT OF MONEY TO TENS OF MILLIONS OF DOLLARS IS THAT THE PEOPLE AROUND YOU DRAMATICALLY CHANGE.*
> — Dave Chappelle

This provocative quote moves beyond discussing the wealthy person *per se*, and focuses on how friends, family and associates of that person are likely to change. According to Chappelle, who undoubtedly speaks from first-hand experience, those people "dramatically" change. The dramatic change is likely to be both positive and negative.

On the positive side, the wealthy person is likely to see and experience friends, family and associates engage in increased deferential behavior. Wealth often confers an aura of power and prestige for those who possess it.

Those in the presence of that aura may act in a more cordial, courteous, and reverential manner than they would towards someone who did not possess that wealth. As funny as Chappelle is, he was probably even funnier to friends and family as his wealth increased.

But there is also a dark side to the dramatic change. Family, friends, and associates may attempt to lobby for special favors and considerations. They may come to you with loan requests, investment opportunities – attention you never expected (or wanted).

Coupled with this increased lobbying is the likelihood of exerting psychological pressure on the wealthy (and understandably hesitant) benefactor. That pressure will be especially strong from immediate family members who feel they are somehow owed a financial favor because of family ties.

Wealth tests the personal values of those who are wealthy and the personal values of those who hope or expect to inherit. As you acquire wealth, don't be surprised when people around you dramatically change.

DEDUCTIBLE

There are two common meanings for deductible: one applies to <u>insurance</u>, the other to income taxes.

A deductible in insurance coverage is the amount you must pay before the insurance kicks in. For example, you may have auto insurance with a $500 deductible. That means that you must pay the first $500 of the loss caused by an accident, but you are insured for all expenses beyond that amount. Health insurance also includes deductibles.

Another definition for deductible relates to income tax preparation. Some expenses are deducted from your total gross income, reducing your taxable income if you itemize. Examples might include interest you pay on your <u>mortgage</u>, charitable donations and high medical expenses.

The 2018 Tax Cuts and Job Act legislation greatly reduced the ability to use tax deductions; most individual taxpayers now take the standard deduction. But the provisions of that act expire in 2025 and changes in tax law prior to that date could alter the situation. Stay tuned.

THE LESSON

There is often a tradeoff between the amount of the deductible and your insurance premium (what you pay for your insurance). The higher the deductible, the lower the premium. If you don't believe you are at <u>risk</u> for making a claim against the insurance company, and if you can afford to pay the deductible if you do make a claim, then in general it is best to increase your deductible and reduce your insurance premium. For taxable deductions, make sure you keep records in case you are audited and must "prove" all your deductions. ♪

> *IF YOU'RE GOING TO PLAY THE GAME PROPERLY,*
> *YOU'D BETTER KNOW EVERY RULE.*
> — *Barbara Jordan*

Although specifying what is and is not deductible is something both insurance policies and tax laws have in common, they also share another characteristic: Both contain numerous rules you must follow to avoid penalties. Failure to follow insurance policy rules can lead to loss of coverage; noncompliance with tax laws can even put you behind bars.

You might interpret the rules to fit your circumstances or challenge them in court. Distraught policy holders sue insurance companies on a daily basis, and vice versa. Similarly, taxpayers have kept tax attorneys handsomely employed ever since the first tax laws were written.

But there is also a heart and soul to these rules, laws and penalties, and Barbara Jordan's quote captures it. Challenging and testing an explicit rule is different than being blind-sided or deceived. We justifiably feel violated if we're penalized for breaking an unknown, non-existent or hidden rule.

Fine print and exclusionary clauses in insurance policies may drive you crazy, but at least the rules are in print. Tax laws and the contingency clauses that support them may also make you nuts, but at least they are written laws, not IRS secrets designed to play "gotcha" with *your* money.

Apply Jordan's wisdom in your daily life. You want to be treated fairly by others, be they friends, family or co-workers. You deserve to know the rules of the game. So do others, who expect the same fairness and knowledge of the rules from you.

Because the object of the game is getting through life, the rules are simple: equity, honesty, transparency, and consistency. If you violate these rules, playing "gotcha" with other people, you will be the one who loses.

Play the games, know the rules, and apply the rules fairly.

ESCROW

Escrow refers to money (usually) or property that is handed over to a third party for safekeeping while two other parties complete their transaction.

For example, if you own a house, you – party #1 – will owe taxes and <u>insurance</u> to the municipality and insurance company – party #2 – at a time in the future. Until that time, you transfer money temporarily to your bank or <u>mortgage</u> company – party #3 – to hold until payments are due. The third party makes the payments.

Here's another example: Suppose you buy something on the internet from a stranger. If you pay before receiving the goods, you may worry that you won't actually receive them. On the other hand, the seller might refuse to ship the goods without being paid first. In such cases, a trusted third party can alleviate all the uncertainty by receiving the goods *and* the payment.

Basically, escrow ensures that one or both parties can fulfill their sides of a transaction without any anxiety or fear of loss.

THE LESSON

Using a trusted third party to handle escrow will give you, and the second party, a little peace of mind. Recognize the fears of those with whom you are doing business and use escrow when you have any doubts. Do your homework and make sure the third party holding the escrow can be trusted. Does that party have a proven track record of fulfilling obligations? Escrow is a common practice in real estate transactions. Be aware of contingencies in a buy/sell agreement and recognize that either party could lose money placed in escrow if contingencies affecting them are not met.

> ## DON'T WAIT FOR TROUBLE.
> ### — Chuck Yeager

On Oct. 14, 1947, U.S. Air Force Captain Chuck Yeager, sitting at the controls of a supersonic jet, the Bell X-1, became the first man to break the sound barrier. Needless to say, he and his ground crew did everything humanly possible to ensure that his aircraft would surpass Mach 1 without killing him. He and his crew did not "wait for trouble."

Yeager's simple, yet profound, advice has two life lessons: Control what you can control and choose optimism over pessimism.

There is much we cannot control. Yet what we can do is realistically assess a situation and control what we can control. Will there still be surprises? Threats and possible failure because of unknown risks? You bet! That's one of life's defining qualities – uncertainty about tomorrow.

Yeager and his crew used the best information they had to prevent trouble. Not a bad strategy for you to follow, regardless of the threats you face.

Yeager was not crazy. He was not on a suicide mission; he was on mission to break the sound barrier – dangerous but calculated. He and his crew believed it could be done and were optimistic that they would.

Control what you can and choose optimism over pessimism. Sound advice for life generally and prudent advice for managing your personal finances specifically.

Escrow accounts reflect both lessons. They help you control what you can control and make possible the optimism you need to seal the deal.

FORBEARANCE

Sometimes, you just cannot make a required payment on your <u>mortgage</u>, your student loan or your credit card. If you cannot, ask your lender for forbearance, in which case the lender may allow you to postpone (not eliminate) one or more required payments.

Forbearance is temporary relief from short-term financial hardship. Often, but not always, forbearance will come with a price – added interest payments and/or higher future payments – but the price will be less than <u>foreclosure</u> (losing your property) or <u>bankruptcy</u>.

Lenders offer different forbearance terms to different borrowers. If your lender grants you forbearance, be sure you can, and will, meet the terms of the agreement.

Many lenders offered forbearance programs during the COVID-19 crisis, when unprecedented numbers of Americans were furloughed or lost their jobs altogether.

THE LESSON

If you are facing short-term financial difficulty, don't hesitate to ask your lender for forbearance. It's better than actually defaulting on your required payment. It's relief. It's a safety net. Even better, receiving forbearance does not always adversely affect your credit score. Granting forbearance on a mortgage payment may also make sense to the lender; there are significant costs associated with foreclosure.

FORGIVENESS IS THE FINAL FORM OF LOVE.
— Reinhold Niebuhr

Arguably, love is the most frequent theme in poems, songs, books and movies. At some point in your life, you probably told someone "I love you," and someone probably expressed the same feeling to you.

But even if you have yet to share that emotion with another, you almost surely long for the day when you will. To love and to be loved is a basic human need.

Because of its transcendent power to elevate our humanity and its power to create endearing bonds with families and friends, Niebuhr's quote deserves our attention.

We all know what love looks like and feels like when the sparks first fly. We show our affection through soft-spoken words, affectionate glances, tender touching, and possibly heartfelt gifts. Depending on the depth of our love we may even say "I will always love you."

But life is hard and unpredictable. The sparks may turn into dying embers. The one we love may hurt us, possibly more than we ever could have imagined. What then should we feel? Anger? Betrayal? Hate? Retribution?

Niebuhr offers a different choice: forgiveness. By framing forgiveness as "the final form of love," he is telling us that if we truly love someone, we will show it not just when the sparks first fly and not when the one we love meets our needs. If we truly love someone, we will forgive when it tests our humanity, when it is most difficult to forgive.

We hope your love for another is never tested. But if it is, realize that your feelings of anger, hate, betrayal and retribution are predictable. You have the choice to move beyond those emotions to forgiveness – that "final form of love."

FORECLOSURE

If a borrower misses one or more payments on a collateralized loan, the lender will first send a notice of the missed payment(s). A lender will usually try to work with the borrower to remedy the situation. If that doesn't work, the lender may legally force the sale of the <u>collateral</u>. This process is known as foreclosure.

Foreclosures are mostly associated with <u>mortgages</u>, when the property serves as collateral. Before the collateral is sold, the courts usually give the borrower several chances to repay the loan. The entire foreclosure process may take one or two years to settle. Sometimes even longer.

If the sale of the collateral fails to bring in enough money to pay off the loan balance, the borrower may be forced to make up the difference. This is called a "deficiency."

THE LESSON

Always try to pay off your loans. If you fall into temporary financial difficulty, ask for <u>forbearance</u>. A foreclosure on your property should be avoided whenever possible. It will stay on your credit report for many years, reducing your <u>FICO</u> score and damaging your <u>Five C's of Credit</u>. A foreclosure can trigger considerable stress, affecting your mental and physical health. If that happens, get help right away. If your car or house is being repossessed, don't make the problem worse by breaking the law.

A foreclosure is a lose-lose outcome. The borrower loses a home, jeopardizes his credit rating, and may incur legal costs. The lender loses future interest payments and incurs administrative and legal costs as well. The lender will probably sell the property to recoup his losses, but that sale price may not make him whole.

Aside from both parties' financial losses, they will also experience emotional costs that test heart and soul. Losing a home is a traumatizing experience; the borrower will likely need a long time to recover.

On the flip side, lenders take no joy in foreclosing. They understand the drama, trauma, and implications of taking away someone's hearth and home.

As heart-wrenching as this scenario is, those who lose a home to foreclosure still have a path to healing and happiness: a "reservoir" of "resilience," as Brown described it, proving to the self and the world that tomorrow will be better than today.

Loss defines an outcome. It does *not* define you as a person. You are not a loser because you suffered a defeat or a loss. A tragedy becomes more tragic if you fail to learn, adapt and move on – the essence of resilience.

At some time, you – indeed, everyone – will experience the heartbreak of failure, defeat, and loss. Move on and look back at the loss as a test that made you stronger. Losers are those who fail to find the resilience to move beyond the loss.

Finally, realize that resilience can, and must, be built up over time to create a "reservoir of emotional strength" when you need it. Your friends and family help you build that reservoir.

Help them to build theirs.

FSA (FLEXIBLE SPENDING ACCOUNT)

Many employers will offer a flexible spending account (FSA), a nice fringe benefit that you should always take advantage of, but with some attention.

An FSA allows you to make contributions to pay for many medical expenses, including deductibles, co-pays, prescriptions, medical equipment and travel for medical purposes, using pre-tax dollars.

So, as your taxable income declines, so does your federal income tax.

There is a limit as to how much you can contribute each year to your FSA. In 2020, the limit was $2,750, but it varies from year to year.

Here's why you should pay attention to it: As you contribute to your FSA, you must "use it or lose it." If you fail to spend the amount you contribute, the unspent amount is forfeited. Some virtuous employers will allow the FSA a grace period of as much as 2.5 months *in the subsequent year* to spend a contribution; still others will allow as much as $500 of the unspent amount to be carried over to the subsequent year. Look into whether your employer offers this very useful benefit.

A "dependent care FSA" is different account with different rules. You can use it to pay for certain childcare expenses and care for qualifying adults who meet specific rules established by the Internal Revenue Service.

THE LESSON

Take advantage of an FSA if your employer offers it, but carefully estimate your projected medical expenses. You do not want to lose the money you contribute, which you will if your medical expenses fall short of your estimate. If you underspend at the end of the year, including any grace period, you may want to splurge on bandages, prescription eyeglasses, reading glasses, sunscreen and other approved medical "equipment" that can be paid by your FSA contribution. Visit the FSA store at **fsastore.com** to see what you can buy with your unspent FSA contributions.

> ## MANY RECEIVE ADVICE,
> ## ONLY THE WISE PROFIT FROM IT.
> ### — Harper Lee

At some point in your life, you were given advice, either because you asked for it or because someone thought you needed to hear it "for you own good."

What Harper Lee is telling us has profound implications that go well beyond the legal and administrative issues of an FSA. The issue is not the specific advice or whether it was solicited. The issue is, were you wise enough to "profit" because of it?

Did the advice help you become better? Did you change a behavior that needed to change? Did you carefully examine what you did and why you did it?

Some people ponder the advice, carefully considering its pros and cons. They even probe issues they may find confusing to make sure they fully understand its pros and cons. They also consider the source of that advice, determining if it is offered in good faith and not self-serving.

Those who ponder and consider are open minded. They will "prosper" because of that advice, regardless of the decision to accept, reject or "sleep on it."

Others, though, give knee-jerk responses, either pro or con, to the advice:

"I don't understand it; this doesn't make sense to me."
"I don't trust you."
"Of course! I'll do whatever you say."

They don't critically consider and ponder the advice; they accept or reject based on biases, prejudice or fear. They are the unwise who will never "prosper." They are no longer thinking critically.

Finally, the heart and soul of any advice is not just the advice itself, but the heart and soul of those offering it, and of those receiving it.

We wish you heart, soul, and wisdom in giving advice, and receiving advice.

PENSION PLANS

In a pension plan, you and/or your employer contribute for your retirement.

There are two types of pension plans: defined contribution and defined benefit. A defined contribution plan, such as a 401K, allows you to choose investments.

A defined benefit plan is a traditional pension plan. You and/or your employer contribute to the plan, but your employer chooses investments. When you retire, you get an <u>annuity,</u> an income stream for the rest of your life.

If a pension plan is "qualified" (defined by the IRS), your contribution reduces your taxable income today. There are limits to the annual amount you can contribute to a pension plan. Often, your employer will match what you invest, i.e., if you invest 4 percent of your salary, your employer might match it and add another 4 percent. Employer matching is basically a 100 percent <u>rate of return</u> on your investment.

Recently, problems have emerged for many defined benefit plans; employers have failed to contribute enough to pay the promised benefits. In other cases, they invested inappropriately and lost money. Fortunately, the Pension Benefit Guaranty Corporation (PBGC) insures the retirement benefits of many workers in the private sector to certain limits. But it does *not* insure pension plans in other sectors such as state and local municipal pensions and plans offered by most religious institutions.

THE LESSON

Defined contribution plans are becoming the norm. If you invest in <u>stocks</u> that do well, you will do well in a defined contribution plan. If you are young – under 40 – you should invest almost entirely in stocks. Throughout the history of our great country, stocks have *always* outperformed fixed-income securities over long periods of time (30-plus years). As you age and approach retirement, become more conservative and allocate more of your portfolio to fixed income. Beware: you will have to pay the IRS a 10-percent penalty if you withdraw money before age 59½. We are not fans of going into debt, but borrowing at, say 6 percent, to get a 100-percent return (from your employer match) is good, productive debt. Avoid the bad debt, like borrowing for an unnecessary and unaffordable vacation.

> *IT IS BETTER TO LIVE RICH THAN TO DIE RICH.*
> *— Samuel Johnson*

You contribute to a pension plan for a simple reason: to receive monthly income when no longer employed. Budgeting and cutting costs during retirement means your pension should hopefully suffice.

But Samuel Johnson, a literary giant, offers a provocative take on living, dying and "richness." Regardless of your age – and regardless of your proximity to retirement – you should consider the implications of that advice.

On one hand, you could interpret Johnson as saying, live your life so that spending your last dollar coincides with taking your last breath. You have often heard others paraphrase that interpretation: You can't take it with you, so enjoy it while you're here. Maybe you have said this yourself.

Indeed, you should enjoy your money while you are here. But enjoying your richness implies defining rich in more than strictly financial terms.

For example, consider these synonyms for richness: abundance, bountiful, ample, fertile, full. Johnson's guidance gets to the heart of viewing richness beyond dollars.

You could be financially wealthy while psychologically and emotionally bankrupt. You have money, but you are not living "richly." You are spending, but not enjoying.

Don't assume that the only reason retirees volunteer is to fill up their time during the day. Yes, it helps them occupy their time, but more importantly it adds richness to their lives. That richness provides things their monthly pension can't buy – meaning, purpose, fulfillment and a bountiful life.

If you are retired, live richly regardless of your monthly income. If you are contributing to a pension plan, make bountiful living part of that plan.

None of us can take it with us when we die. But we all have the power to leave behind a priceless legacy far more valuable than money. Living richly creates that legacy.

IRAS: TAX-DEFERRED INVESTING

Traditional individual retirement accounts (IRAs) are like 401K plans, encouraging you to save for retirement. And they should, for two reasons:

First, you will pay less taxes today. Put $1,000 into a traditional IRA; if your tax bracket is 25 percent, then you will pay $250 less in taxes this year. Second, you also will pay no taxes in every subsequent year until you retire on all of the interest, dividends and capital gains you earn on your IRA investments.

These features are called "tax deferral." "Deferral" is the key word. You will pay taxes after you start withdrawing money, which can occur without penalty beginning at age 59½. You must start withdrawing money from your traditional IRA after you turn 72. (Check this age requirement; Congress changes it from time to time). These withdrawals are called required minimum distributions (RMDs), and are taxed as ordinary income. IRS tables spell out your RMDs; most brokers will do it for you. Be sure to obey the RMD rules; the IRS will penalize you if you don't.

If your tax bracket is the same in retirement, or lower, you will come out ahead because of the benefits of tax deferral. We present an example in the notes.

There is another type of IRA: the Roth IRA. Contributions to it are *not* tax deductible; they do not lower your tax bill when you contribute. But interest, dividends and capital gains earned in your Roth IRA investments are never taxed. Better still, the withdrawals from your Roth IRA are never taxed! You never have to make withdrawals from a Roth IRA; your beneficiaries will inherit it tax-free. Just be sure to follow the rules for Roth IRAs.

There are other tax-deferred plans such as 529 plans, which can be used for educational expenses, for anyone, including yourself.

THE LESSON

If you are in a low tax bracket today, the Roth IRA is typically the best option. The higher your current tax bracket, the more likely the traditional IRA will be better. Always know the rules when contributing to any IRA or tax-deferred investment; the IRS will penalize you with higher taxes if you don't follow them. If you are unsure, talk to your financial advisor or carefully read and understand the rules online. ♪

> *BE CAREFUL NOT TO COMPROMISE WHAT YOU WANT MOST FOR WHAT YOU WANT NOW.*
> *— Zig Ziglar*

Deferral simply means delaying or putting off. If you think about it (and we do want you to think about it), you decide every day about what you can and cannot defer – what must I do now, and what can I put off until later.

Your pattern for deferring is probably what most people do: You delay the trivial and you delay what's uncomfortable, both physical and emotional.

But there is another pattern. Some (not all) of us also defer those things that are pleasurable, positive and gratifying, not because we are martyrs or masochists, but because we believe in the value of the ultimate payoff. We forgo something good today to obtain something better tomorrow.

We give up dessert to lose weight. We give up relaxation to exercise and gain stamina and health. We give up personal time to meet needs of our family and friends. We give up "good-time" spending to save towards our financial goals.

In fact, delaying gratification may be the single most important factor in your quest for financial and personal fulfillment. That discipline means you move from wishing and hoping to planning and executing. It means you can say "no" when part of you would rather say "yes." It means your financial goal is not to hit the lottery.

Ultimately it means you achieve your goals because you were willing to pay the price. If we are willing to learn, life is always ready to teach. One of its lessons is everything has a cost. The cost for what you want most is giving up what you want now.

VESTING

Vesting is a legal term meaning that you own something. It is commonly used in the context of employee benefits. Employers impose vesting periods to keep you motivated and committed to the company.

Employers may contribute benefits for your retirement plan, but you may not be vested in your plan for several years. (Seven years is not uncommon.) That means that you have to work for your employer for that "vesting period" before you legally own the company's contributions, but you will always own your own personal contributions. Even after you vest, your employer may add additional work requirements until you can withdraw the funds.

Employee <u>stock options</u> may also have a vesting period. If so, you are required to work for your employer for that period before you own and can exercise your rights to buy shares of <u>stock</u> at the specified price. Similarly, some companies will reward key employees with "restricted stock" – shares of stock that you cannot sell until you vest, or until you or the company satisfy some stated goals.

Vesting also applies to last wills and testaments. Some stipulate a vesting period before the <u>assets</u> of the deceased are distributed to the beneficiaries.

THE LESSON

Vesting period can be like golden handcuffs. You may want to leave your employer for a new job, but since you have not yet vested, you will probably stay where you are. If it is a matter of months, then it may be an easy decision to stay. But longer periods require careful, and personal, cost-benefit analysis. How important is it to be unhappy in your current job, perhaps working for a boss you dislike, to vest in your employer's retirement benefits? But just as there are golden handcuffs, there are golden opportunities. You may have an opportunity to leave a job you like for one you will like even more. The cost-benefit analysis of your vesting options with your current employer will then come into play.

> *IN THE FIRST EIGHT OR SO YEARS AT MICROSOFT, WE WERE ALWAYS CHAINED TO OUR TERMINALS, AND AFTER I GOT SICK THE FIRST TIME, I DECIDED THAT I WAS GOING TO BE MORE ADVENTUROUS AND EXPLORE MORE OF THE WORLD.*
> — *Paul Allen*

Few companies change the world; still fewer company founders become industry icons. Microsoft and its founders, Bill Gates and Paul Allen, are among the exceptions.

Allen's personal statement about his early years at Microsoft teaches us three important lessons:

First, he and undoubtedly other initial employees felt chained to their terminals, but those chains were gold plated. They made the decision to devote herculean efforts and countless hours to build a company they felt could change the world. Their commitment paid off in ways none of them could have imagined – for the world and for them. The lesson: Commitment is always voluntary; sacrificial commitment is driven by purpose.

Second, Paul Allen was diagnosed with Hodgkin's lymphoma in 1982, and that diagnosis spurred him to question his devotion to Microsoft relative to what he might lose. The lesson: Gold-plated chains lose their luster when you see your life slipping away.

Third, Allen decided to be more "adventurous" and explore the world. He wasn't removing the chains to live as a victim, bemoaning his diagnosis and waiting to die. To the contrary, he removed the chains and became an adventurer, an explorer and a philanthropist.

The lesson: When confronted with your mortality, stop making excuses for not doing what you want to do. Carpe Diem - seize the day.

Purpose, recognition of our mortality and living your dream, powerful lessons indeed. A computer programmer who changed the world created his own "program" because of those three lessons.

Thank you Paul, for your talent, passion, and philanthropy, and may you rest in peace.

INSURANCE

Because living carries inherent risks, and unfortunate outcomes are always a possibility, insurers provide a variety of policies to mitigate the risks: life, medical, auto, homeowners, renters, long-term care, long term disability and personal liability. Your premiums pay for coverage in case you need it for any of those potential losses, providing a financial safety net. When you buy that safety net you also buy peace of mind.

Always examine the ratings of your insurance companies. If your insurer is not financially sound, it may not have the ability to pay your claims. A.M. Best, Fitch, Moody's and Standard & Poor's are prominent ratings agencies of insurers, but their opinions are not perfect. AIG was a highly rated insurance company just before it collapsed during the 2008 recession and came under government control.

In 2019, the Federal Reserve reported that 18 percent of U.S. adults had unpaid medical bills, and 25 percent failed to receive needed medical care because they felt they could not afford it. Not surprisingly, medical bills are the leading cause of bankruptcy. With health insurance, your bills will almost always be small, and you will get the medical care you need. Medicare exists so that elderly and disabled Americans can get medical care at low cost.

THE LESSON

Insurance is an essential part of your financial plan. More importantly, you need the right kind of insurance to cover your specific risks. As your lifestyle and financial situation change, so will your risks. The right agent concerned with your risks, rather than a sales commission, will align your risks with the right coverage. If your agent does not audit your risk exposures, you have the wrong agent. Carefully consider all that you currently own. What would happen to you if these assets were put at risk? Protect yourself and your family; buy the insurance you need. Also, cancel policies and coverage you don't need.

> *THERE'S NO DISASTER THAT CAN'T*
> *BECOME A BLESSING, AND NO BLESSING*
> *THAT CAN'T BECOME A DISASTER.*
> — *Richard Bach*

Insurance does not protect us from disaster. Indeed, many of our blessings can later turn into tragedy. But it does protect us financially from the consequences of disaster. We may require medical care because of injury, illness or disease. We may suffer the loss of our home because of fire or flood. But if we are insured, we will not suffer the additional disaster of bankruptcy.

Ideally, insurance makes us financially whole following misfortune. Medical bills will be paid; cars can be replaced; houses can be rebuilt. If you ever filed a claim, you were probably glad to have insurance; you may even have felt blessed.

But insurance cannot make us emotionally whole. Being a beneficiary of a life insurance policy does not mean you won't mourn the loss of a loved one. Building a new house may not fulfill the longing for your old house. Medical coverage for major life-threatening surgery will not erase the emotional trauma that made the operation necessary.

It is possible to suffer physically or emotionally and view it later as a blessing in disguise, not because you had financial coverage, but because you have a new appreciation for life. You had *emotional insurance.*

Emotional insurance is the belief you will survive the disaster and be better because of it.

Emotional insurance is the support from family and friends who help you get past disaster.

Emotional insurance is knowing you are a survivor, not a victim.

If you want to be able to file an emotional insurance claim when you need it, start paying your insurance premiums today. Focus on family and friends, on heart and soul.

CAPITAL GAINS AND LOSSES

Capital gains mean that you sold an <u>asset</u> for more than what you paid. You can also have *unrealized* capital gains, which means the price of your asset increases, but you have yet to sell it. By contrast, a capital loss means that the current price of the asset is less than what you paid.

The tax laws on capital gains and losses are complex and always changing. You pay taxes on capital gains and you often, though not always, get a tax break on your capital losses. There are annual limits on the capital losses you can deduct, thus reducing your taxes in a year.

You may or may not have to pay a capital gains tax on your house. If you owned and lived in your dwelling for more than two years, then $250,000 of your capital gains are tax free if you are single, and $500,000 of capital gains are tax free if you are married and file a joint return. However, you can never deduct a capital loss if you sell your home for less than what you paid.

Some sophisticated assets, such as futures contracts (see <u>commodities</u>) and some <u>options</u>, require that you pay taxes on unrealized capital gains. The capital gains tax rate often depends on how long you owned an asset; i.e., the tax rates on short-term capital gains are usually greater than those on long-term capital gains. The government often changes the length of time that differentiates long term from short term.

THE LESSON

Use the tax strategy that minimizes your taxes within the constraints of the tax laws. It is often advantageous to realize short-term capital losses. For example, you may wish to sell one investment at a loss in order to benefit from a tax-<u>deductible</u> loss. At the same time, you may buy a similar investment (but not too similar because of tax laws). Depending on the complexity of your financial life, decide whether to use tax-preparation software or pay for an accountant, and whether to hire a financial planner (<u>financial advisor</u> or wealth manager). Remember to keep good records.

> *THE BEST WAY TO TEACH YOUR KIDS ABOUT TAXES IS TO EAT 30% OF THEIR ICE CREAM.*
> — *Bill Murray*

One way to get a pulse on the emotions and psyche of the American public is to follow the hosts of late night talk shows. Their humor reflects a predictable pattern. You'll hear jokes about politics, the comings and goings of the rich and famous, the day's headlines and, depending on the time of year, the holidays.

There is another predictable pattern. Every year, just before April 15, those same comedians joke about income taxes. If their humor really reflects what many Americans feel, and why they are feeling it, then the uptick in income tax jokes is indeed instructive. It tells us that U.S. tax laws are complex, ever-changing and make fodder for the classic good news-bad news joke: The good news is you made money; the bad news is...."

But there is another explanation for the jokes. Because of their ever-changing complexity tax returns are susceptible to "creative accounting," a connotatively rich phrase if ever there was one. Those late night monologues play off of this phrase and Americans' ambivalence about the fairness of their tax system.

So, keep updated records of your finances. Follow the current tax laws. Be prepared to defend the tax forms you sign. Oh, and never forget Al Capone.

Al was one of the most notorious gangsters of the 20th century; but he didn't go to prison for racketeering, bootlegging, grand theft or even murder.

He was convicted of tax evasion.

BANKRUPTCY

Bankruptcy is a legal proceeding that occurs when an individual, firm or government cannot pay its bills for which it is contractually liable. You can file for bankruptcy if you are overwhelmed by your debt or if you fail to make a payment or multiple payments. The parties to whom you owe money may force you into bankruptcy.

Bankruptcy negotiations are handled in bankruptcy courts. Often, the bankrupt party (the "debtor") can negotiate a reduced payment. Sometimes, the debtor's assets will be liquidated to help pay the debts. The parties who are owed money (the "creditors") often have to settle for receiving less than what they are owed.

The U.S. Bankruptcy Code sets out the different ways bankruptcy is handled, and the rules are set out by the different chapters of the Bankruptcy Code. The chapters present ways that the debtor's "non-exempt" assets might be sold (liquidated) to help pay the unpaid debts or allow a business to continue operating. Individuals usually file under Chapters 7 and 13. Businesses usually file under Chapter 11.

Two related terms are "default" and "insolvency." When you fail to make a scheduled financial payment, such as debt (interest or principal) payment, you are "in default" or "have defaulted." Default often leads to bankruptcy. Insolvency (or "being insolvent") is another term for the inability to pay bills. You can be insolvent, but not yet legally bankrupt.

THE LESSON

Manage your debts so that you don't file for bankruptcy. First, talk to your creditors and see if you can work things out. If you have several different types of debt (multiple credit cards and other loans), debt consolidation combines your debt payments into one loan with one bill, often at a lower interest rate. This may or may not solve your debt problem; get an outside expert opinion before you sign up for a consolidation loan. If all else fails, sometimes bankruptcy will be the last resort. If you do go bankrupt, recognize that the bankruptcy laws exist to help you get back on your feet, but the stigma of bankruptcy will follow you for years, and it could be difficult for you to access credit during that time.

Consider for a moment the language we use to describe bankruptcy, and those suffering its traumatic effects. If bankruptcy is imminent, you are "drowning" in debt. Your debts are "underwater." You are trying to keep your "head above water," but are "quickly sinking."

But examine the drowning/bankrupt metaphor from the perspective of Coelho's insightful quote. You do not drown because you fall in a river. You drown because you go under and are unable to get out; you stay submerged.

Many people fall into debt. Some progress into bankruptcy; others do not. Assuming the debt load is comparable, is there anything that differentiates between those who stay submerged and those who do not? Indeed, there is.

Those who fall into debt and quickly recover are proactive; they aggressively fight to get out of debt. Rather than submerging deeper, they budget, cut out unnecessary expenses and develop a plan for survival. They don't sink until bankruptcy is the only option.

Secondly, they seek out "lifesavers," others who can help pull them out of debt and make sure they stay out. Family, friends, financial advisors, even lenders who are owed the money, can be lifesavers. For those surviving burdensome debt, bankruptcy is not seen as inevitable.

Finally, the drowning/bankruptcy metaphor may also be applied to moral bankruptcy. No one is perfect. We may all engage in unethical behaviors, which are atypical and out of character for us. But those who are morally bankrupt sink even further, unwilling, or unable, to pull themselves out.

Bankruptcy – financial or moral – means sink or swim. We may all fall... but we don't all drown.

FINANCIAL WEALTH

Wealth, of course, is the topic of this book. Most people think of wealth only in terms of money. Add up all your assets that can be sold (i.e., that have value to others), subtract your liabilities, and you will compute your financial wealth (also known as net worth).

Using this definition, the Federal Reserve estimated in 2019 that the "median" wealth for American families – where half of all households fell above, and half fell below – was less than $121,700. The June 2020 Modern Wealth Survey by Charles Schwab, the financial services company, found that Americans believe they need $2 million to be wealthy – down from $2.6 million before the COVID pandemic.

According to the Fed survey, 42 percent of Americans' wealth took the form of financial assets – stocks, mutual funds, retirement and checking accounts. The rest was mostly vehicles, residential and nonresidential property, and business equity.

Not counted in this definition of wealth is the present value of future expected earnings. Adding that makes us all a lot wealthier, but it is speculative and more difficult to measure.

Many financial decision-making models assume that "only financial wealth matters" and that our goal should be to maximize our personal financial wealth (given the amount of risk we are willing to bear). The concept of time value of money defines wealth as what you now own (as in the Fed's definition of wealth) plus the present value of your expected future cash flows.

THE LESSON

We are troubled by the fact that 50 percent of American families have accumulated less than $122,000 in wealth. Even with Social Security, that won't be enough to live on for 20-30 years in retirement. This lack of wealth exists largely because only 59 percent of American families save! If you don't save, it will be difficult to accumulate wealth. Get started saving early and start leveraging your financial literacy today!

You can be wealthy without a penny in the bank, if you have...

Peace
Empathy
Compassion
Health
Wisdom
Happiness
Purpose
Serenity
Family
Manners
Friends
Competence
Integrity
Respect
Morals
Love
Truth
Forgiveness
Time
Loyalty
Gratitude
Confidence
Spirituality
Laughter
Freedom
Dreams
Trust

This is not an exhaustive list, but the point is clear: You don't need money to be "rich." Many individuals with considerable financial assets are unhappy, and wish they were "rich." Be aware of how much wealth you really possess, and what you need to do acquire *total wealth*. And one last thing - periodically revisit the right hand pages of this book!

CHAPTER 5

DUE DILIGENCE IS NOW DUE

DILIGENCE IS THE MOTHER OF GOOD FORTUNE.
— Benjamin Disraeli

You have completed a journey of discovery, a journey exploring *total wealth*: the duality of financial wealth and personal fulfillment. Even though you all completed the journey, you did not all start with the same mindset.

Some of you believed that a harmonious blending of financial security and personal well-being was not only possible, but also chose it as a personal goal. You now have tools for turning that goal into reality and validation that your goal is achievable.

Some of you were open minded to the possibility that *total wealth* could be achieved, but still had doubts. We challenged you to question those doubts and more importantly to open your mind even further. Meeting this challenge will enhance your wealth and your spiritual well-being.

And finally, some of you may have thought the phrase "the heart and soul of financial literacy" was foolhardy at best, and a contradiction in terms at worst. You were more than skeptical; you were questioning whether we really deserved our PhDs.

You undoubtedly believed that money is money, and soul is soul... and never the twain shall meet. You assumed that enrichment at one can only come at the expense of the other. Your journey may indeed have been much more than instructional, it may have touched your soul.

Regardless of your initial mindset, and regardless of the lessons you learned, there is one final lesson that cuts across all the previous lessons in this book: You will only achieve *total wealth* through due diligence.

DUE DILIGENCE AND TOTAL WEALTH

Just as a fool and his money are soon parted, so too is a fool and his family. Due diligence prevents you from becoming that fool. With due diligence you critically assess the risks in building your *total wealth* and develop strategies for mitigating those risks.

Because of previous lessons in this book, you are well aware of due diligence strategies: checking references, obtaining written agreements, protecting personal financial data, following the law, maintaining accurate up to date records, validating information, seeking professional guidance, agreeing to terms only if you understand the terms, and periodically monitoring portfolio performance.

In addition, because of consumer protection laws and industry specific mandates, professionals in the financial services industry are required to disclose the most common financial risks when you sign on their "bottom line." Those disclosures help you and protect them against potential litigation. Unfortunately, some of those disclosures are usually in small print!

But there are other risks which are less obvious, potentially more devastating, and never in print, large or small. Unless you mitigate these risks, you may lose more than money; you may lose your sense of self and your family. These risks speak to the heart and soul of due diligence.

Risk of Procrastination

Throughout this book we stressed the importance of time, your most valuable resource. Time is money; but time is also the basis of personal fulfillment. Proof of the former is in the power of compounding interest. Proof of the latter is in the precious memories of the time spent with your family and friends.

The clock and calendar wait for no one and do not discriminate. While we are alive those minutes, hours and days are available to all of us equally. What we do with that time is a personal choice, and wasting that time is a choice with potentially tragic consequences.

- Waiting until tomorrow to name beneficiaries, draft a will, decide on power of attorney, or draft a living will, could be one day too late.
- Waiting until tomorrow to monitor your portfolio managed by an advisor could be one day too late.
- Waiting until tomorrow to tell family members you love them could be one day too late.

- Waiting until tomorrow to examine your self-defeating investing habits and biases could be one day too late.
- Waiting until tomorrow to contact a creditor who might be threatening to sue or foreclose could be one day too late.

Tips for Conquering Your Procrastination

Own your procrastination and its consequences. If you sense you have a problem procrastinating, you *do* have a problem. If you believe someday is one of the seven days in a week, you are living in a delusional dream world. Wake up now!

Focus on the big picture: *total wealth*.

Set specific, achievable intermediate goals.

Prioritize your goals. Without prioritizing, everything is important, and nothing is important. Think about this. You may believe there will always be enough time to make amends or fix a mistake. Stop believing it. You are not guaranteed that time.

Create reminders with apps or on a written calendar.

Work with peer groups for mutual support in achieving your goals.

Reward yourself for achieving goals.

Change your self-defeating, internal monologue from "I'll do this tomorrow" to "I'll do this today."

Start with the most difficult tasks first.

Stop seeing time away from work as a cost and start seeing time with family as an investment.

Google the phrase "end of life regrets." You will find multiple references to regretting not what we did do but regretting what we did not do.

Vin Scully had a 67-year broadcasting career with the Brooklyn & Los Angeles Dodgers. In reminiscing about his legacy and age he said, *"It's a mere moment in a man's life between an All-Star game and an old-timer's game."* Control procrastination and you will not regret losing those "moments."

Risk of Hubris

Bill Gates on the problem with success: *"Success is a lousy teacher. It seduces smart people into thinking they can't lose."* The seductive power of success goes go even further. Successful investors may start believing they are entitled to and worthy of their good fortune.

Indeed, overconfidence is one of the most prevalent behavioral biases that investors display, leading to poorer investing performance. Overconfident investors may then start acting superior towards others, with an aura of condescension, smugness, entitlement, and omnipotence, the most common traits of hubris.

Once we start arrogantly believing that we are better, smarter, and omnipotent, and once we act on those beliefs, we are guilty of hubris.

Enron's bankruptcy and subsequent convictions of Ken Lay, Jeff Skilling, and Andy Fastow is a dramatic example of the devastating consequences of hubris. Were they smart? Of course they were. Were they financially successful? Indeed. Were they seduced by that success? Have no doubts. Did their hubris ruin lives? Tragically it did …. thousands of lives.

The risks of hubris are tragic not only for you but also for those who love you, and trust you, the potential casualties of your belief you can't lose.

The Antidotes for Hubris

Open yourself to honest, candid feedback about how others see you. Don't shoot the messenger if you don't like the message.

To paraphrase Harry Truman, the buck stops with you. Share the credit for your success with others; accept the responsibility for loss. It has been said that the reason that many individuals use brokers is that when they do well, they take credit for themselves, and when they don't do well, they can blame their brokers.

Listen more than you talk.

See humility as a strength, not a weakness. If you think you are indispensable, think again. Cemeteries are filled with indispensable people.

Understand that money does not define your wealth, only your portfolio.

Accept that you are worthy not because of what you possess, but because of what you share. The Judeo-Christian and Islamic faiths speak to the duty one has to help others in need.

Donate to worthy causes … anonymously.

Acknowledge your family as partners in your success. Your family members are your partners in building your portfolio, even though they never signed contracts. Thank them.

What you *are* is ultimately more important than what you *own*.

Model yourself after those you admire, not those who you think are rich. When you follow their model, you will view your good fortune as a promissory note to others...you will start paying back.

Risk of Nepotism

Recall our discussion of the AGENCY CONFLICT. As you build *Your Total Wealth*, you are likely to buy insurance, seek financial advice, make investments, hire an attorney, and possibly hire a therapist and or life coach.

Ask yourself a basic question before hiring any of these agents: Is this person or organization ethical, competent, and worth my trust? Then ask yourself a follow up: Am I hiring this person because they are a family member? If the answer to the second question is "Yes," proceed with considerable caution.

Is it possible, that a family member could be a competent financial advisor and fiduciary? Of course it is. However, it is also possible that a family member serving as your agent would have a conflict of interest.

Financial planning reduces to a basic trade off: risks vs rewards. The risk of having a family member as your agent may not be worth the reward of relying on family. If something goes wrong, even if it is out of your family member agent's control, the fallout may taint your feelings towards that relative, and vice versa.

It ain't worth the risk. Better that it be an independent 3rd party. Families have been ripped apart because of misunderstandings and financial returns that did not meet expectations. Tragically, some families have been ripped apart across multiple generations!

Conflicts of interest with a family member serving as an agent are more problematic than conflicts created by an agent who is not a family member. The former conflicts may reflect a long history of emotions and family discord affecting the agent's recommendations. The latter conflicts reflect a more basic problem: decisions affecting the client driven by the agent's portfolio, not the client's portfolio.

Also, the family member serving as agent may be named as a beneficiary on the account or may be related to a beneficiary. An agent who is also a beneficiary of an account, directly or indirectly, would have to have the wisdom of Solomon and the purity of Mother Theresa to manage the account without some self-serving interest.

Reducing the Risk of Nepotism

There is a valid reason why surgeons choose not to operate on family members. Offering an opinion, yes. Holding the scalpel, no. Emotional attachment clouds judgments and distorts objectivity.

As your portfolio increases in size and complexity seek guidance outside the family. If your family member is a financial services professional, never hesitate to confer with outside counsel anyway, for a second opinion.

Risk of Never Enough

Don't feel guilty about wanting more. There is nothing wrong with wanting to increase your financial wealth or your personal fulfillment. We seek wealth and we seek fulfillment; those are predictable human pursuits. If they were not predictable, we would not have written this book.

The risk is not in wanting more. The risk is failing to appreciate what you already have and feeling unfulfilled regardless how much you have. Enough *is* enough for many reading this book, and enough may *never* be enough for others. When wanting more becomes an insatiable need, *total wealth* is an impossibility.

Trying to feed an insatiable need means that you are constantly striving, but never thriving. You are making money but not enjoying it or what it can buy. You want more, and need more, in a never-ending cycle of striving more and thriving less.

The underlying problem of never having enough is that material possessions may be a proxy for filling a need that cannot be filled by material possessions or online contacts. Compulsive eaters, spenders, adulterers, and hoarders are examples of those trying to fill an underlying insatiable, emotional need.

Unless you accept the risk of never having enough you will have a hunger that will never be satisfied.

The Remedy for Never Enough

Experience the value of having less. One of the positive outcomes of the 2020 Covid-19 pandemic is that many were forced to appreciate the basics: health, safety, and family. Because of limited travel, shopping, and eating out, you may now appreciate the simple truth that less is more.

If physical possessions are no longer making you happy, change course and strive for spiritual fulfillment. Religion and spirituality mean different things to different people. Regardless of how you define it, your pursuit should be peace, contentment, and reverence for values beyond physical needs.

Stop comparing yourself to people who you think have more than you do. That comparison will be never ending and always leads to jealousy and heartache. Besides, you might be surprised to learn they wished they had what you have.

Stop regretting what you don't have and start rejoicing in what you do have.

Volunteer.

Spend time watching children play.

Stop focusing on *what* you want to achieve and begin focusing on *why* you want to achieve it.

If striving is preventing you from thriving, and it's affecting your physical and mental health, seek the counseling of a life coach or a therapist.

—

"Due diligence is the mother of good fortune" because like all mothers it nurtures protects and defends. You deserve to achieve your goals of financial and personal enrichment. Just listen to your "mother."

CONCLUSION

When you die, the final test of how you lived your life will not be the size of your financial portfolio. It will be the legacy you created while you lived – the innumerable decisions resulting in that priceless portfolio of *total wealth*.

Your legacy will be the memories your family and friends will have for the rest of their lives, memories about you and your relationship with them.

Life is short, but legacies endure. We wish you wisdom and compassion in creating those memories and that legacy – a legacy that defines you as one who lived a life balancing your financial wealth with heart and soul.

NOTES

Our goal was to simplify financial concepts without creating undue complexity. We also felt that some readers might want a more detailed or nuanced discussion of terms, especially, those based on quantitative analysis. The notes that follow provide that discussion. We've also included references for further exploration if you want to build upon and increase your financial literacy and its relationship to heart and soul implications.

Good news...there is no test...except in the day-to-day application of your financial literacy!

1. Research Study of Financial Planners:

Our study of 1374 financial planners discussed in the Introduction, was presented in two articles. The first included rationale, methodology, data analysis and conclusions. See:

Dubofsky, David, and Lyle Sussman, 2009 "The Changing Role of the Financial Planner Part 1: From Financial Analytics to Coaching and Life Planning", *Journal of Financial Planning* 22, 8 (August), 48-57.

The second discussed the coaching and counseling skills required of financial advisors:

Sussman, Lyle, and David Dubofsky, 2009, "The Changing Roles of the Financial Planner Part 2: Prescriptions for Coaching and Life Planning", *Journal of Financial Planning* 22, 9 (September), 50-56.

2. Finance:

Want to learn more about the basics of finance? Visit:

https://www.usnews.com/topics/author/coryanne-hicks

https://napkinfinance.com

Two influential books about Finance, and you don't need a business or math degree to enjoy and learn from them:

A Random Walk Down Wall Street, 12th edition, by Burton G. Malkiel. W.W. Norton & Company publishers, 2020.

Stocks for the Long Run, 5th edition, by Jeremy J. Siegel. McGraw-Hill Education, 2014.

3. The SEC:

The SEC requires publicly traded companies to provide and release accurate information about themselves, so that all investors get access to it at the same time. To understand the reason for this requirement, see https://www.sec.gov/edgar.shtml .

The SEC listens to investors. If you have a complaint, let them know: https://www.sec.gov/complaint/select.shtml .

Insider trading only became illegal with the passage of The Securities Exchange Act of 1934. It was passed because of the role of insider trading in causing the 1929 stock market crash and Great Depression. The SEC has successfully prosecuted several prominent individuals for insider trading, including Martha Stewart, Michael Milken, Jeffrey Skilling and Steven A. Cohen.

4. Computing the Time Value of Money:

Define PV as present value, and FV as future value. If you begin with PV and you earn an annual interest rate of r%, compounded annually, then after N years, you will have a future value of FV = $PV(1+r)^N$.

For example, if you have $100 today and you invest it to earn 5%/year, for twenty years, at the end of the 20th year, you will have $100(1.05)^{20}$ = $265.33 = FV.

You can also "discount" a future amount back to today, by rearranging the formula: PV = $FV/(1+r)^N$ = $FV(1+r)^{-N}$. So, suppose you want to have $1 million when you retire 40 years from today. If you can earn 6%/year, then how much must you invest today? The answer is PV = $1,000,000/(1.06)^{40}$ = $97,222.19.

5. Compounding Interest:

The following graph shows four different savings plans, over a 50 year period. Line 1 shows how your savings will grow if you deposit $100 today at 5%/year, over a 50-year period; your $100 will grow to $1146.74. Line 2 shows that if you can increase the rate of return to 6% per year, your $100 will grow to $1842.02. Increasing your rate of return by just 1% (100 basis points) increases your final wealth by over 60%.

Line 3 shows the impact of more frequent compounding. For example, if you earn an annual rate of 6%, *compounded monthly*, your final wealth grows to $1993.60!

Finally, the lesson of line 4 is to start saving early. It shows the impact of delaying your $100 investment by just five years. If you wait to start saving until year five, and earn 5%/year, your final wealth will only be $898.50.

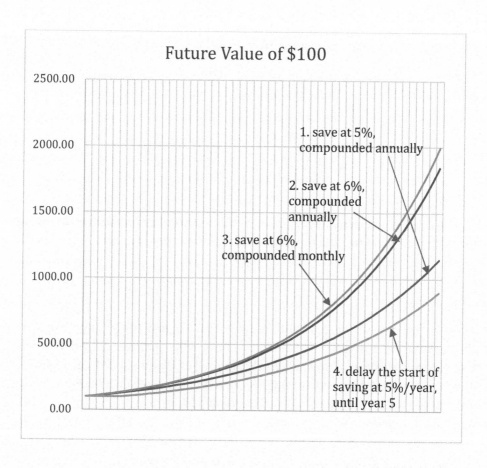

Future Value of $100

1. save at 5%, compounded annually

2. save at 6%, compounded annually

3. save at 6%, compounded monthly

4. delay the start of saving at 5%/year, until year 5

6. Rate of Return:

Computing a rate of return is complex when you have a long holding period, you have made several transactions during the holding period (made more than one purchase and sale) or received several dividends.

But for short holding periods with one dividend, you can compute the simple holding period rate of return (R) with this formula:

$$R = \frac{P_1 - P_0 + Div}{P_0} = \frac{P_1 - P_0}{P_0} + \frac{Div}{P_0}$$

Where P_1 = the price at the end of the period; the selling price

P_0 = the beginning price; the purchase price. Note that $P_1 - P_0$ is the capital gain.

Div = the dividend that you receive. Note that Div/P$_0$ is the dividend yield.

For example, suppose you buy a stock for $50/share. A year from now you sell the stock for $55/share. Also, during the year, you get a $1 dividend per share. Your rate of return is 12%:

$$R = \frac{55 - 50 + 1}{50} = \frac{6}{50} = 12\%$$

Visit https://financeformulas.net/Total-Stock-Return.html for further discussion of the formula including a simple calculator for the formula.

7. Efficiency:

Given its prominence, it is hard to believe that Eugene Fama only coined the phrase "efficient markets" in 1970 (Fama, Eugene F., "Efficient Capital Markets: A Review of Theory and Empirical Work", Journal of Finance, 1970, pp. 383-417). His seminal work led to the first index fund, the Vanguard 500 Index Fund, which was created in 1975. Prior to 1975, all mutual funds were actively managed with high fees. Fama won the Nobel Prize in Economics in 2013. Efficient markets are very important to the SEC. Its mission states: ... to protect investors, maintain fair, orderly, and efficient markets, and facilitate capital formation."

See https://www.sec.gov/Article/whatwedo.html .

8. Diversification:

The graph below shows that risk (measured by the dispersion or standard deviation of your annual rates of return) declines as you randomly add more stocks to your portfolio. On average the risk of one stock is 0.50. The risk of a ten-stock portfolio is only 0.25; i.e., ten stocks cuts your risk in half, on average.

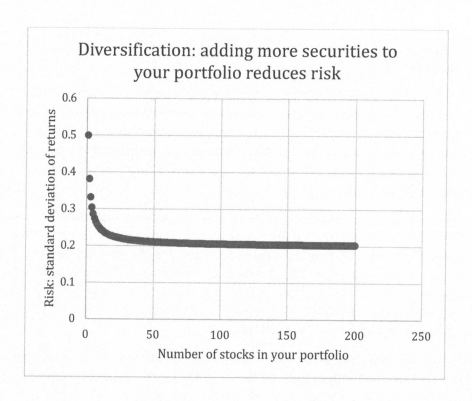

Diversification: adding more securities to your portfolio reduces risk

Risk: standard deviation of returns (y-axis, from 0 to 0.6)

Number of stocks in your portfolio (x-axis, from 0 to 250)

9. Derivatives:

There are many websites that can teach you about derivatives. We recommend you start with the Khan Academy:

https://www.khanacademy.org/economics-finance-domain/core-finance/derivative-securities

The Bank for International Settlements (BIS) provides a great deal of data concerning the size of the derivatives markets:
https://www.bis.org/statistics/

10. Cryptocurrency:

There are many websites that discuss using and/or investing in cryptocurrencies, and their underlying blockchain technologies. See, for example,

https://www.benzinga.com/money/is-bitcoin-a-good-investment/, and

https://www.khanacademy.org/economics-finance-domain/core-finance/money-and-banking/bitcoin/v/bitcoin-what-is-it .

11. Index Funds:

We wrote that perhaps the primary advantage of investing in index funds and index ETFs is their low expenses. But there are some index funds that charge outrageously (in our opinion) high expense ratios. We don't understand why any investor would ever invest in them. If it is because their financial advisor put them there, they need a different financial advisor. If it was their own decision, they need a financial advisor.

For example, there is a large S&P500 index fund that has a very low expense ratio of 0.015%. An expense ratio of 0.015% means you should expect to underperform the S&P500 index by 0.015% each year. Thus, if the rate of return on the S&P500 index is 13.99 (which was the actual rate of return on the S&P500 in the ten years ending June 30, 2020), you might expect to get a rate of return of 13.975% on this low expense ratio S&P500 Index Fund. It turns out that during that decade, you would have earned 13.97% in this fund!

But other S&P500 index funds have higher expense ratios. Some are **very** high. There is actually one with an expense ratio of 2.41%! In the ten years ending June 30, 2020, the S&P500 index returned 13.99% per year, while this particular S&P500 index fund returned only 11.22% per year!

The graph below shows how $100 invested in two different S&P500 index funds on June 1, 2010 would have fared over the ten-year period (121 months) ending August 31, 2020. You would have ended up with $386 in the low expense ratio index fund, but only $302 in the S&P500 index fund with a 2.41% expense ratio. Let us stress again…. both funds hold exactly the same portfolios.

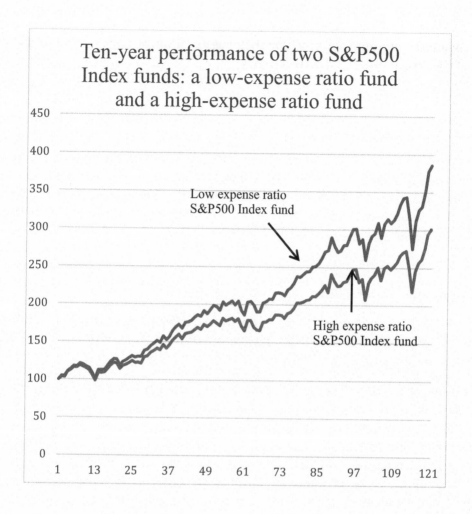

Ten-year performance of two S&P500 Index funds: a low-expense ratio fund and a high-expense ratio fund

Low expense ratio S&P500 Index fund

High expense ratio S&P500 Index fund

Leveraged index funds (2X and 3X funds, and inverse funds) have peculiarities that you *must* understand before using them. So much so that the SEC issued a special warning about them; see sec.gov/investor/pubs/leveragedetfs-alert.htm.

The statistics cited concerning index fund assets were obtained from the Investment Company Institute at http://www.ici.org .

12. Mutual Funds Selection:

Many services provide ratings for mutual funds, including Morningstar and Value Line. When comparing funds, you must compare apples to apples. Thus, you cannot compare the performance of a stock fund to a bond fund. You cannot compare the performance of a fund that invests only in large cap stocks to one that invests only in small cap stocks.

Morningstar rates funds from gold (the funds they believe are the best) to silver to bronze to neutral to negative (the worst). Value Line rates funds from 1 (the best funds, in their opinion) to 5 (the worst).

Research indicates that the worst performing and poorest ranking funds (Morningstar negative and Value Line 5) tend to continue to perform poorly in subsequent years. The primary reason is their high expense ratios. Thus, avoid the worst performing, lowest ranked funds. And always examine the expense ratios of funds before you invest.

13. Expected rate of return:

The expected rate of return is, in a sense, the most likely rate of return you could realize when you own a security. But the ACTUAL rate of return you will earn might be anything.

You may have seen the bell-shaped curve shown below. It describes the probability of an event when it is "normally distributed." In in this case the event is the rate of return for the S&P500 stock market index. The vertical axis is the probability of an outcome, and the horizontal axis displays the different outcomes. The peak of the bell is the expected return, 12%, which is the actual average annual rate of return for owning the S&P500, including reinvested dividends, between 1926 and 2019. However, note also that the probability of getting 12% is only about 2.1%, or once every 48 years. The probability that you will get 12% or more is about 51%. The probability that you will lose money (a negative rate of return) is about 25%.

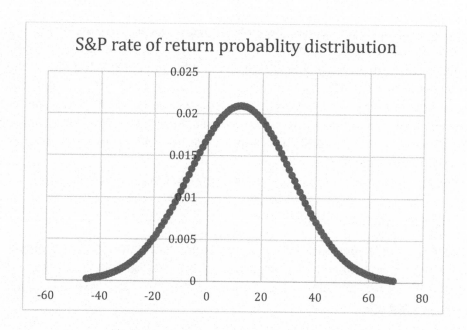

S&P rate of return probablity distribution

Consider this analogy: remember when the weather forecasters told you that tomorrow's high temperature is expected to be seventy degrees? The actual high may turn out to be anything between 65 and 75 degrees.

14. FICO:

Fair Isaac is a publicly traded company. While many parties (including Fair Isaac) advertise that they'll tell you your FICO score for a price, several credit cards will provide you with your FICO score for free. Check out https://www.doughroller.net/credit-cards/credit-cards-that-offer-credit-scores/

15. APR:

We mentioned in our APR discussion that there are times that borrowing at a lower APR will cost more than borrowing at a higher APR. Similarly, there are times that lending at a lower APR will benefit you more than lending at a higher APR. The reason for these cases is the frequency of compounding, which determines the EAR (recall that the EAR and APY are the same thing).

For example, suppose you are offered the opportunity to borrow $10,000 at a 12% APR, compounded monthly, or to borrow $10,000 at a 12.1% APR, compounded semiannually. The EAR of the first loan is 12.68%. The EAR of the second opportunity is 12.47%. Borrowing at the 12% APR will cost you more than if you borrow at the 12.1% APR! If your loan will be repaid with 12 monthly payments, your monthly payments will be $888.49 with the 12% APR loan, and $887.58 with the 12.1% APR loan. The lesson: use EAR's (APY's) to compare borrowing rates, not APR's.

16: Legal information:

https://www.nolo.com is an excellent source for legal information on several topics we cover, such as living will, power of attorney, guarantor, cosign, and bankruptcy. They provide a legal encyclopedia at https://www.nolo.com/legal-encyclopedia .

17. Finding a Financial Advisor:

The following list is a good place to start. They are also not affiliated with any brokerages or investment companies:

www.smartasset.com

www.nerdwallet.com

www.bankrate.com

www.financialtherapyassociation.org is an association of financial planners who specialize in combing financial planning with personal and family therapy.

18. Financial Fraud:

Because of the significance and pervasiveness of fraud generally, and financial fraud specifically, we recommend the following sources as a follow up to our Yin and Yang:

Dan Ariely, *The Honest Truth About Dishonesty,* 2013, Harper Perennial, New York.

John R. Boatright, ***Ethics in Finance, 3rd edition***, 2014, Wiley-Blackwell Publishers. Provides an excellent introduction into illegal and unethical behavior in the finance industry.

19. Deductible:

Don't confuse a deductible with a co-pay or co-insurance. A co-pay is a fixed dollar amount that you must pay a doctor *after* you have paid your doctors an amount equal to the deductible. You make co-pays *after* the deductible is reached. For example, suppose your deductible is $500 and your co-pay is $50 per doctor's visit. You must pay all your medical expenses until you reach the $500 threshold. Subsequently, you pay $50 every time you visit a doctor.

Co-insurance is similar to co-pay, except that it is a percentage of your medical cost. Co-insurance is financially risky. If you have 20% co-insurance, and you have a $50,000 medical bill, you will have to pay $10,000! To protect against this outcome, pay attention to your "out-of-pocket maximum," which is a cap on the medical expenses you will pay in a year. Often, you will have deductibles, co-pays and co-insurance. All are out of pocket expenses until you reach your out-of-pocket maximum.

The government offers a glossary of healthcare and insurance terms at https://www.healthcare.gov/glossary/ .

20. IRAs: Tax-deferred investing

The following example illustrates the long-term benefits of tax deferred investing:

Assume that you invest $4000/year in a typical taxable mutual fund or ETF that generates an 8% annual rate of return in taxable income. You will get $320/year before tax. If you are in the 25% tax bracket, you will get to keep $240/year after taxes. If you reinvest this $240/year, then when you retire, 40 years in the future, you will have $619,048.

Suppose instead you invest $4000/year in that same mutual fund, but in a traditional IRA. This will reduce your taxes by $1000/year. Invest that additional $1000 in tax savings back in your IRA. Thus, you save $5000/year ($4000 of your own money plus $1000 thanks to Uncle Sam's generosity). You get your 8% annual return, but won't have to pay any taxes until you retire, 40 years from today. In 40 years, you will have $1,295,283! Unfortunately, you will owe taxes. If you withdraw everything and pay your 25% in taxes, you are left with $971,462.

With the IRA, you end up with $352,414 more in retirement! This windfall occurs because you defer taxes on your traditional IRA contributions and on your IRA earnings.

This may not work as well if you are in a higher tax bracket in retirement than you were while you were working. Also, some individuals must pay more for their Medicare benefits depending on their retirement income.

Few individuals take out their entire IRA in one lump sum at retirement. Most take out the required minimum distributions (RMDs) which must begin after you are 72 years old. The initial RMDs start out at about 4-5%/year of your IRA investment account value. If your IRA balance is $1,295,283, your first RMD will be about $52,000 in the year after you turn 72. RMDs exist because the IRS wants its tax revenues.

Relatedly, a common question retirees ask their financial advisors is, "how much of my investment account can I safely spend each year?" Our response is if you are very conservative (risk averse) and are under 80 years of age, just divide the balance in your investments by the number of years of life you think you have remaining. If you are 70 and think you'll live to be one hundred, spend 1/30, or 3.33%, of your account balance. Chances are you can afford to spend more (a common rule of thumb is 4%), but recognize that the more you spend, the greater the chance you will run out of money sooner than you like. The downside of prematurely running out of money is worse than leaving money unspent on the table. Your retirement account RMDs will be greater than 3.33%, so you may consider re-saving some of your RMD in a taxable account.

INDEX

D

E

Public Company Accounting Oversight
Board 24

pump and dump 128
put 21, 40, 66, 81, 96, 117, 134, 139, 151, 154, 178

Q

quotes 5, 46, 86

R

rate of return 34, 36, 37, 44, 48, 54, 57, 58, 78, 84, 94, 96, 100, 104, 112, 114, 128, 148, 174, 175, 176, 178, 180, 183
real estate 12, 46, 60, 72, 110, 112, 114, 115, 116, 118, 132, 134, 135, 140
real estate investment trusts 72
recession 22, 30, 62, 100, 154
refinancing 114, 118, 120
registered investment advisors 126
REITS *See* real estate investment trusts
required minimum distributions 150, 184
rescission 118
restricted stock 152
revenues 16, 18, 21, 98, 184
RIAs *See* registered investment advisors
risk 10, 14, 16, 30, 38, 44, 54, 55, 56, 58, 60, 61, 62, 63, 64, 65, 68, 70, 71, 74, 78, 82, 86, 95, 96, 100, 101, 104, 105, 106, 107, 108, 128, 132, 133, 138, 154, 160, 167, 168, 176, 184
risk averse 62, 82, 184
risk aversion 30, 58, 62, 63, 82
risk aversion questionnaire 62
risk premium 56
RMD *See* required minimum distribution
ROA *See* return on assets
robo-advisor 124
ROE *See* return on equity

rule of 72 34

S

S&P 500 Index 68, 70, 78, 80, 88, 94, 178
S&P EWI 84
Satoshi Nakamoto 74
SEC *See* Securities and Exchange Commission
Securities and Exchange Commission 24, 40, 126, 192
security deposit 134
sell short 72, 90, 91
short squeeze 90
simple interest 34, 112
spread 18, 26, 46, 58, 66, 86
Standard & Poor's 54, 154
standard deviation 60, 62
stock exchange 26, 27
stockholders' equity 10
stock 1, 8, 10, 16, 22, 24, 26, 27, 30, 38, 40, 44, 46, 48, 50, 54, 56, 58, 60, 62, 64, 68, 70, 72, 76, 78, 80, 81, 82, 84, 86, 88, 90, 92, 95, 96, 98, 104, 116, 128, 148, 160, 176, 180
sunk cost 50
swap 64

T

tangible 12, 13, 42, 57, 87
target date funds 82
time is money 164
time value of money 32, 33, 160
TIPS *See* Treasury Inflation Protected Securities
Treasury bill 42, 54, 56, 114
Treasury Inflation Protected Securities 28

ABOUT THE AUTHORS

David Dubofsky, PhD, CFA

Dr. David Dubofsky has published over 40 articles in journals including <u>Journal of Finance</u>, <u>Journal of Financial and Quantitative Analysis</u> and <u>Journal of Money, Credit and Banking</u>. He is the author of <u>Derivatives: Valuation and Risk Management</u> (co-authored with Tom Miller), and <u>Options and Financial Futures: Valuation and Uses</u>. Prior to retiring in 2020, Dr. Dubofsky held faculty and administrative positions at the University of Louisville, Texas A&M University, Virginia Commonwealth University, TCU Neeley School of Business and Seattle University. Previously, he was a visiting academic scholar for the Office of Economic Analysis at the U.S. Securities and Exchange Commission and worked for Nalco Chemical Company and Standard Oil of Indiana. He earned his PhD in Finance from the University of Washington, MBA from the University of Houston, and BE in Chemical Engineering from City College of New York. He is a CFA® charterholder.

Lyle Sussman, PhD

Dr. Lyle Sussman is the former Chairman and Professor of Management and Entrepreneurship, University of Louisville, and Professor Emeritus. He previously taught at the University of Michigan and the University of Pittsburgh. Aside from 65 scholarly articles, he is a bestselling business author with more than 1,000,000 copies of his books in print in 15 languages. Excerpts of his books have appeared in *Harvard Business Review Updates, Savvy, Bottom Line Reports, Working Woman, Inc., Success, Executive Book Summaries, Investor's Daily, CNN, American Banker, US Air In Flight Audio*, and hundreds of management blogs. He has spoken to more than 100,000 people and consulted around the world for both the private and public sector, with significant impact in the banking industry. He received his PhD from Purdue University, and his BS and MS degrees from University of Wisconsin-Milwaukee. He was selected for Who's Who in Business Higher Education (Academic Keys).

Visit our website: www.Yourtotalwealth.com

We will continue to add tips, news, and updates, at this site to help you achieve your financial goal without sacrificing personal fulfillment. This site also provides a simple way to contact the authors.

If you would like to order multiple copies for your personal or professional network with your personal imprint, let us know. We can make that happen.